Becoming Human Again

Recovering the Ten Words for a Dehumanized Age

Dr. David Phillips

ENNOVO
PRESS

Becoming Human Again: Recovering the Ten Words for a Dehumanized Age

Printed in the United States of America

ISBN: 979-8-234-02055-0

First Edition
March 2026

For more information, visit:
www.wdavidphillips.com

Contents

Preface

This is the book I've wanted to write for over a decade.

In 2011, I set out to write about the life of Christ—not out of a desire for another theological treatise, but out of a pastoral alarm. I feared we were substituting Jesus with "gospel" and "truth"— noble words, biblical words, but dangerously abstract when detached from the One they point to.

Leonard Sweet captures this sharply in an article entitled "Cheap Gospel, Weak Christ. Restoring Christ's Supremacy": "Christians have made the gospel about so many things ... things other than Christ. Jesus Christ is the gravitational pull that brings everything together and gives them significance, reality, and meaning. Without him, all things lose their value. Without him, all things are but detached pieces floating around in space."[1]

Years earlier, my thinking had been impacted by an event that happened at a Shoney's Restaurant in Huntsville, Alabama. I was with a couple of friends from college and, during our meal, we spent much of the time expressing our frustration with the church. On our way out, a man, who happened to be from out of town, stopped us and explained to us that during that entire meal, we had mentioned Jesus a total of zero times. We talked around Him, but did not mention Him. And that event changed my thinking about the danger of talking about everything but Jesus.

So I have long thought the church had turned language about Jesus into substitutes for Jesus himself.

At the end of the day, what matters most, what matters only, is Jesus. And I would discover that this same prophetic concern lies at the heart of the Ten Commandments, not as static rules, but as words spoken by the One who is Life, and as rhythms meant to tether our hearts back to Him.

Now, that first project had a different tone than most of what I typically write. It was lighter, more narrative, more reflective. Normally, I lean toward depth, detail, explanation. I want to trace every theological thread, examine every textual nuance. I love that kind of work. But I also knew that depth doesn't always equal clarity. And clarity, especially when writing about Christ, matters deeply.

So I started it. I wrote a lot. I edited it. I invited a few friends to read it. They offered generous and wise feedback. But I never released it. Life moved on. And yet, as often happens, the writing stayed with me. It shaped me. It formed something in me. Because when you spend time writing about Jesus, He becomes more real. And the more real He becomes, the more you begin to see the brokenness within yourself—and the more He transforms you.

That experience also changed how I wanted to write.

I live in a technological world. I work in it too. I've been fascinated by technology since I was a kid. And I use it, enthusiastically, for everything from research to organization to, yes, even writing. I don't see that as a threat to faith, but as a tool, something that, when used carefully, can serve the process of reflection and discovery.

Some time ago, I heard something in a sermon that gave me pause. The speaker said something like: "The Ten Commandments aren't just prohibitions; they reflect the core of what it means to be human." That line stuck with me. It lodged in the back of my mind and caused me to do what my late dad used to call "ciphering." And this book is, in many ways, an outgrowth of that ciphering.

I did what I often do: I asked questions. I turned to Scripture. I listened to voices wiser than mine. I even opened up a conversation with AI. I asked if there was any theological validity to the idea that the Ten Commandments reveal not just divine law but human design. I asked what patterns in Scripture might support it. I asked whether any authors had explored it before.

The responses were fascinating. Not flawless, but suggestive. Helpful. Thought-provoking. They pointed me toward deeper study, and eventually, back toward writing.

So I began again.

I dusted off the style of that unfinished Christ-focused manuscript and tried it on once more. Surprisingly, it fit. Not perfectly—but well enough to help me write with greater clarity and freedom. Some of that original content guided me here. And it reminded me, all over again, of the power, sufficiency, and centrality of Jesus Christ.

That's been my heart all along. It was the heartbeat of my doctoral dissertation back in 2009: to help people rediscover how humanity was originally designed, and to point toward how we might live more fully into that design on this side of Heaven.

The Ten Words arrive later in the book—after we have sat with the question of what humanity was designed to be, after we have walked through the ruin of empire and the grace of covenant. The commandments land with more weight when we have first understood what we were made to reflect.

There are other ideas that may grow from this. I suspect more will come. But for now, I offer you this first piece.

It is personal. It is prayerful.

And above all, it is for Jesus.

I've long loved a song written by Chris Tomlin and sung by Christy Nockels that captures the prayer of my life—even when I fail to live up to it. These words have become an anchor and aspiration:

Let it be Jesus
The first name that I call
Let it be Jesus
My song inside the storm
I'll never need another

For me to live is Christ
For me to live is Christ
God I breathe Your name
Above everything
Let it be, let it be Jesus

Let it be Jesus from the rising of the sun
And let it be Jesus when all is said and done
I'll never need another
Jesus there's no other

Should I ever be abandoned
Should I ever be acclaimed
Should I ever be surrounded
By the fire and the flame
There's a name I will remember
There's a name I will proclaim
Let it be, let it be Jesus

Yes. Let it be Jesus.

David Phillips

Villa Rica, GA

Notes

1.https://web.archive.org/web/20250911053809/https://
preachitteachit.org/articles/cheap-gospel-weak-christ-restoring-
christs-supremacy/amp/

Hearing the Voice Again

"The voice of the Lord is powerful; the voice of the Lord is full of majesty."

— Psalm 29:4

There is a Voice that spoke before the world fell silent.

A Voice that shaped mountains, stirred oceans, carved law into stone, and whispered mercy into dust.

It is a Voice that humanity has struggled to hear—and often feared to obey.

We live in a world of echoes. A world where the memory of true humanness flickers like a half-forgotten dream. In our striving, our hoarding, our endless building of towers and empires, we have not become more free; we have become more lost.

The old ache remains: Who are we? Whose are we? What does it mean to be truly alive?

Long ago, amid thunder and flame, God spoke Ten Words to a people barely free, a people trembling at the foot of Sinai.

Ten Words to teach them how to be human again.

Ten Words to carve paths of worship, honor, truth, and joy into the hard soil of fear and forgetting.

But the Ten Words were never meant to be stone monuments to a vanished covenant. They were—and still are—the living grammar of a life awakened by grace.

This book is an attempt to listen to those Words afresh.

Not as relics of ancient religion.

Not as a checklist of duties to grimly fulfill.

But as a living, breathing call to remember who we are and to whom we belong.

Along the way, we will walk through empire and wilderness, through the deformations of sin and the hopes of covenant, through the brokenness of our modern world and the glories of Christ's resurrection.

We will see how the Ten Words name our inhumanity—and call us out of it.

We will see how they find their true voice not in our efforts but in Jesus Christ, the Word made flesh.

We will see how, in Christ, these commandments are not burdens but promises—promises of a life made new.

This is a book for pilgrims.

For the weary and the hopeful.

For those who have tried to build a life out of noise and performance and who have found it wanting.

For those who hunger to hear the Voice again.

Come and listen.

Come and remember.

Come and begin the journey home.

CHAPTER 1

SIGNS OF THE HUMAN

"The Word became flesh and made his dwelling among us."

— John 1:14

A Child Learning to Read

She was five years old, and the book smelled like summer—like dust and old paper warmed by afternoon light. Her mother had placed it in her small hands, and the weight of it surprised her. It was heavier than she expected, this thing called a book, with its cardboard spine and pages that whispered when she turned them. The pictures were beautiful: a rabbit sitting in a garden, a house with blue shutters, a tree with apples hanging like ornaments.

But then her mother pointed to the marks below the pictures. Black lines and curves. Some stood up straight. Others bent and looped. Some clustered together like tiny birds on a wire.

"These," her mother said softly, running her finger under the marks, "are letters. And these letters make words."

The child stared. At first, they seemed random. Meaningless. Just marks on paper. Why would anyone make marks like that? Why not just show the picture and be done?

But her mother was patient. Day after day, she pointed and spoke. "This is A. This is the sound it makes. Here—can you see the letter A in the word apple?" Slowly, impossibly, a transformation began. The marks were no longer random. They had shapes. They had names. They had sounds. And when the sounds linked together— c-a-t, r-a-b-b-i-t, t-r-e-e—something miraculous happened. The marks meant something. They pointed beyond themselves, to a rabbit that hopped, to a tree that grew, to a world larger than the page itself.

One day—she would never forget this moment—she was looking at a page, and suddenly the marks became transparent. She could see through them. She could see the rabbit itself. She could hear the word in her mind before she even spoke it. The marks were no longer barriers between her and meaning. They were windows into it. The marks were signs. They pointed. They opened doors.

"I can read," she whispered to herself, stunned by the simple miracle of it. She was holding meaning in her hands.

What she was discovering—though she had no words for it yet— was the nature of signs themselves. A sign is not arbitrary. It is not the thing itself, but it points beyond itself. It creates a bridge between the visible and the invisible, between the mark and the meaning. Without signs, the world would be chaos—pure sensation, unreadable. But creation is not chaos. It is full of meaning. And meaning is always carried in signs.

This is the great insight that Christian faith has always known: God has written meaning into creation. Not everything is a blank page. The universe is not random noise. Creation itself is readable —if we have eyes to see and ears to hear. A sunrise means something. A storm means something. A bird's song, a human face, a moment of forgiveness—these are all signs. They all point beyond themselves to the character and intention of the God who made us.

And this is where the Ten Words come in. They are not arbitrary rules handed down by an arbitrary God. They are signs. They are marks on the page of human existence, pointing beyond themselves. When we learn to read them rightly, we discover not a list of prohibitions, but a map—a description of how the world actually is when it is aligned with God's intention. We discover that the world, when lived according to these signs, becomes readable, navigable, human.

A World Full of Signs

Stop for a moment on your daily commute. Look at the signs around you. A red octagon means stop. A yellow diamond means caution. A green arrow means go. These signs do not merely describe reality. They actively shape how we move through the world. They protect us. They guide us. They make shared space possible. Without these signs, the intersection would become dangerous chaos. With them, thousands of vehicles and people move through safely each day, each party understanding the same meaning in the same marks.

Or think of a wedding ring. It is metal—gold or silver or platinum. Nothing particularly special about the metal itself. You could find the same material in a piece of jewelry from a pawn shop. But the wedding ring is not just metal. It is a sign. It means covenant. It means promise. It means "I have bound my life to another's." When a person sees that ring on a stranger's hand, they understand something profound about that person's commitments and identity. The ring does not create the marriage —the vows do—but the ring carries the meaning forward through time and space. It speaks without words.

A nation's flag is another example. It is only fabric—cotton or polyester, stitched together in a pattern of colors. But when you see that flag, you do not see mere fabric. You see history. You see sacrifice. You see the hopes and struggles of millions. You see identity. Some will weep at the sight of their nation's flag because the flag carries meaning far beyond what the material itself contains. The sign points to something invisible but utterly real: belonging, memory, honor.

Consider music notation. On a page, it is just dots on lines. Five horizontal lines, and on them sit circles and ovals and stems. To the untrained eye, these markings are meaningless doodles. But to someone who can read the signs—who understands that certain lines and spaces represent certain pitches, that certain symbols mean loud or soft, fast or slow—those marks on the page become Beethoven's Ninth Symphony. They become Bach's Goldberg Variations. The signs do not make the music exist, but they carry it across time. They make it transmissible. A composer who lived three hundred years ago can still speak to your heart today through these signs.

This is the fundamental truth about signs: they create meaning. They make shared understanding possible. And when we honor the signs, when we learn to read them rightly, we build a world of flourishing. But when we ignore the signs, when we distort them or teach others that they are meaningless—the result is always the same: the meaning collapses. The structure of shared reality breaks down.

Christianity, at its deepest level, is what scholar Leonard Sweet calls "a sign religion."[1] God does not operate primarily through abstract propositions or philosophical arguments. God communicates through signs. When Abraham needed to know that he was called, God showed him a sign: a burning bush that blazed but was not consumed. When the Hebrew people were enslaved in Egypt, God gave them a sign: a pillar of fire by night and a pillar of cloud by day. When the resurrection had happened, the disciples were given a sign: an empty tomb. Empty space, absence—a sign that overturned everything they thought they knew about death itself.

And the ultimate sign? The Incarnation. God became human. "The Word became flesh and made his dwelling among us." Jesus Christ is the sign that interprets all other signs. He is what the universe has been pointing toward all along. In him, the invisible God becomes visible. The infinite enters the finite. The sign becomes flesh.

The Ten Words as Signs

For centuries, the Ten Commandments have been read as rules. Rules imposed from above. Rules to follow or face punishment.

This is not wrong, exactly, but it misses something essential. The Ten Commandments are not primarily a legal code. They are a sign-system. They are a coherent set of meaning-markers that describe what reality looks like when it is aligned with God's intention.

Consider the first commandment: ***"You shall have no other gods before me."*** What is this sign pointing to? It is not arbitrary. It is not a whim of a jealous deity. This sign points to the fundamental truth that God alone is ultimate. God alone is infinite. God alone is worthy of the total allegiance that the human heart naturally seeks to give to something. When this sign is honored—when we recognize God's uniqueness and sufficiency— we are aligned with reality as it actually is. We are free from the exhausting search for another ultimate. We are home.

Or take the Sabbath: ***"Remember the Sabbath day, to keep it holy."*** What does this sign point to? It signs that time is not mere utility. It signs that human beings are creatures, not machines. We are made for rest. We are made for rhythm. We are made for relationship with God that exists apart from productivity. When the Sabbath sign is honored, it opens a space where we can remember who we really are. When it is broken, we are trapped in the illusion that we are only what we produce, that our worth is measured in output.

"You shall not murder." What is this sign pointing to? It signs the irreplaceable worth of every human being. Each person—the powerful and the powerless, the beautiful and the broken, the useful and the seemingly useless—bears God's image. Each life is sacred. When this sign is honored, a society that values human dignity becomes possible. When it is broken, when human beings are treated as expendable, as mere obstacles or resources to be exploited, inhumanity spreads like a contagion.

"You shall not steal." This sign points to the justice of God. It signs that property and boundaries and the fruits of one's labor matter. It signs that stealing is not merely taking a thing; it is a violation—a semiotic violation. It is a sign that says "the other person's work and worth do not matter." When this sign is honored, a just community becomes possible. When it is broken, trust dissolves and communities fragment.

"You shall not covet." This sign points to something even deeper. It signs the sufficiency of God's provision. It signs the poison of envy. When we covet—when we obsess over what belongs to another, when we convince ourselves that we need what we do not have in order to be complete—we are living against reality. We are calling God's provision inadequate. We are fracturing our own souls. When this sign is honored, contentment becomes possible. When it is broken, a restless, grasping, never-satisfied culture of consumption emerges.

And this pattern holds true for each of the Ten Words. Each is a sign. Each points beyond itself to the nature of reality and the character of God. Each, when honored, contributes to the flourishing of a community. Each, when broken, introduces a kind of semiotic collapse—meaning drains away, and inhumanity rushes in to fill the void.

Think of it this way: the Ten Words are like the road signs we mentioned earlier. They don't create the road; the road was already there. But they mark the road. They say: "This is the way. Walk here and you will find yourself in a place of safety and flourishing." They guide us. They protect us. They make shared journeying possible. When we ignore them, we do not prove our freedom. We prove our blindness. We crash ourselves and others in the dark.

This is the central claim of this book: the Ten Words are a comprehensive sign-system that describes human life as God designed it.[2] Each commandment is like a single stroke in a vast painting. Viewed individually, you might not understand what you are looking at. But when you step back and see all ten together, when you see how they interconnect and support each other, a portrait emerges. And the portrait is humanity. This is what it means to be made in God's image. This is the shape of a human life, fully alive.

Reading the Signs Rightly

The problem is that we have forgotten how to read the signs. Or worse—we have been actively taught that the signs are meaningless.

Imagine teaching a child that the letters in the book mean nothing. Imagine telling her that the marks on the page are purely subjective, that they do not actually point to anything, that any meaning she finds in them is just her own projection. What would happen? At first, she might try to keep reading. But eventually, she would give up. Why spend time deciphering signs that lead nowhere?

This is what our culture has done. We live in an age of what we might call "semiotic confusion." We have been trained—by advertising, by social media, by a kind of cultural background radiation of distraction and noise—to treat signs as though they mean nothing (or only what we want them to mean). Every image we see, every message we receive, is crafted to manipulate us into believing that what matters most is efficiency, productivity, consumption, and personal preference. These are the only "signs" that get attention. Everything else is sentiment or superstition.

Theologian Walter Brueggemann calls this the "royal consciousness"—the way of thinking that empires impose on their subjects.[3] The royal consciousness does not argue that signs are meaningless; it teaches a different set of meanings. It teaches that the only signs that matter are the signs of power and accumulation. It teaches that the human being is defined by what they produce and consume, not by their image-bearing nature. It teaches that time is a resource to be exploited, not a gift to be received. It teaches that some lives matter and some do not, depending on their usefulness to the system.

This consciousness is designed to suppress the signs. It is designed to keep us from reading the commandments rightly, because if we read them rightly, we will recognize that the system itself is built on lies. If we honor the Sabbath, we threaten the logic of total productivity. If we refuse to covet, we undermine the engine of consumption. If we recognize the image of God in every human being, we make it impossible to exploit, dispose of, or dehumanize anyone. The royal consciousness needs the signs to remain unread.

But here is the good news: the signs endure. They keep speaking, even to a culture that refuses to listen. The Sabbath still whispers—in the exhaustion of the overworked, in the hunger for silence and space, in the occasional moment when we step off the treadmill and remember what it feels like to simply be. The commandment against murder still insists—in the persistent human outrage when injustice occurs, in the movements for dignity and equality that arise again and again, in the conscience that will not be finally silenced. The signs are written into the fabric of our being. We cannot escape them, even when we try.

Learning to read the signs rightly is therefore an act of prophetic vision. It is an awakening to what is true. It is saying to a culture drunk on noise: "Be still. Listen. There are signs written into creation. There is a deeper reality beneath the surface of things. And when you learn to read these signs, you will discover who you actually are."

This is the task of the church. This is the task of this book. We are not offering you new rules or stricter morality. We are offering you a chance to learn to read again. To see again. To recognize the signs that God has written into creation and covenant. To align your life with reality as it actually is—not as the empire tells you it is, but as God has made it to be. This alignment is what we call becoming human again.

What Lies Ahead

This book is structured as a journey through the Ten Words, understood as a sign-system pointing to the full vocation of human beings.

In Chapter 2, we will establish what the signs were designed to point to: the full meaning of human vocation. We will explore what it means to be made in God's image. We will ask: what is a human being? What are we for? What is the shape of a fully alive, fully human life? The Ten Words only make sense when we first understand what a human being is meant to be.

In Chapters 3–5, we will trace what happened when the signs were shattered. We will look at sin, not primarily as a list of individual transgressions, but as a fundamental rejection of the signs themselves—a semiotic rebellion against God's design. We will see how empires are built on the systematic distortion of signs. And we will discover how God's covenant works: not as punishment imposed from outside, but as a rescue operation from within—God's endless attempt to restore his people to reading the signs rightly.

Chapter 6 is where we pause and take a deep diagnostic breath. Here we will read each of the Ten Commandments not as abstract ideals, but as mirrors. Each will become a diagnostic tool: Where do we see this sign broken in our world? What inhumanity results? We will name the ways that the breaking of each sign leads to a kind of semiotic collapse—the draining away of meaning, the corruption of community, the loss of our humanity.

Chapters 7–11 will trace the path of restoration. Here we will ask: How do we live by the signs in a culture opposed to them? How do we resist the seduction of the royal consciousness? How do we form holy imagination—the ability to see the world as God sees it? And how do we discover that the Ten Words, far from being a burden, are a liberating gift that leads us toward becoming fully human? Finally, we will see how all the signs find their fulfillment and interpretation in Christ—the Living Word who came to show us what humanity looks like when it is perfectly aligned with God.

But we are getting ahead of ourselves. For now, return with us to that image of the child with her book. She is sitting in the afternoon light, holding meaning in her hands. She does not know yet what she will discover. She does not know that in learning to read, she will learn to see. That in understanding signs, she will understand the world. That in following the marks on the page, she will find her way home.

Soon she will read her first word. Then her first sentence. Then her first story. And when the marks on the page become words, and the words become worlds, nothing will ever be quite the same. She will see with new eyes. She will understand what she could not before. She will be awakened to meaning.

Come, then. Let us learn to read. Let us discover the signs that God has written into the world. Let us align our lives with reality as it is meant to be. Let us become human again.

Notes

1. Leonard Sweet, *Giving Blood: A Fresh Paradigm for Preaching* (Grand Rapids: Zondervan, 2014). Sweet's semiotic approach to communication frames the Christian message as "EPIC": Experiential, Participatory, Image-rich, and Connective. See also his *Nudge: Awakening Each Other to the God Who's Already There* (Colorado Springs: David C Cook, 2010).

2. Patrick Schreiner, *The Kingdom of God and the Glory of the Cross* (Wheaton: Crossway, 2018), 19–22. Schreiner argues that the kingdom is meant to be seen and not merely believed, that it has a visual and embodied dimension essential to discipleship.

3. Walter Brueggemann, *The Prophetic Imagination*, 2nd ed. (Minneapolis: Fortress Press, 2001), 1–19. Brueggemann distinguishes between the "royal consciousness" that numbs and the "prophetic imagination" that awakens.

Chapter 2

Created for Glory

"And God saw everything that he had made, and behold, it was very good." – Genesis 1:31

The sculptor arrives before dawn. The workshop is cool and still, dust motes floating in the first light that slants through the north-facing window. His hands know this place—every shelf, every tool, the particular smell of stone and linseed oil. He moves without hurrying, without the flourish of someone performing for an audience. This is the private part, the part before the world sees.

He stands before the block. It is unremarkable—limestone, pale and unrevealing. But he sees something in it. Not sees, exactly. Knows. There is a form waiting there, locked in the stone, and his work is to find it and release it. Before his hands touch the chisel, the image is complete in his mind. He has walked around it, studied it from every angle, held it in his consciousness like a prayer.

The first cut is careful. Deliberate. The stone dust rises in a small cloud. He works for hours—cutting, stepping back, seeing, cutting again. The rhythm is hypnotic. The stone gradually yields its secret. A face emerges. A shoulder. The gesture of an arm. What was hidden becomes visible. What was potential becomes actual.

When it is finished, he steps back. The light has moved across the workshop. The figure stands where the stone stood, and it bears the mark of his hands, his vision, his intention. He runs his fingers along the cheekbone. He studies the eyes. And then—almost unconsciously—he does something remarkable. He names it. He speaks a word, a name, and gives the work its identity. The craftsman and his creation are bound together now in that utterance. This is his.

This is how Genesis describes the making of humanity. Not as an afterthought. Not as a byproduct of impersonal natural forces, raw material for labor or exploitation. But as the most intimate act of all creation—dust gathered up in hands that know exactly what they are doing, breath breathed in with intention, and something entirely new brought into being. A creature who would be, in some mysterious way, a living reflection of the One who made him. Not a machine. Not a tool. A beloved work, given a vocation, named into being.

In the Image of God

The foundational truth of Christian anthropology lies in seven words at the beginning of Genesis: "So God created mankind in his own image, in the image of God he created them; male and female he created them." This is not a peripheral truth. This is the center. To understand the Ten Words, to understand sin, to understand redemption, you must begin here.

The image of God has been interpreted many ways throughout the church's history. Some have said it is our reason—the capacity for logic and abstract thought that separates humans from animals. Others have pointed to our soul, our moral capacity, our ability to love. These interpretations have their place, but they miss the primary meaning. The image of God is not primarily about what humans have—not a feature to be catalogued or measured. It is about what humans are called to do. It is a vocation.

In the ancient Near East, kings would place statues of themselves in territories they ruled—images carved in stone, bearing the king's face and form. These were not mere decorations. They were physical representations of the king's presence and authority in that place. To see the image was to see the king. To honor the image was to honor the king. The image signified rule.

When God placed humanity—"the image"—in creation, he was doing something extraordinary. He was making humanity his representatives, his viceroys.[1] Humanity was placed in the garden to rule, to steward, to bring God's wise and loving order into creation. The image is not an ornament. It is a commission. You bear the image of God the way an ambassador bears the seal of the kingdom he represents. Your authority comes from someone else. Your purpose is to extend someone else's rule.

This transforms how we understand human worth. In a world obsessed with productivity, achievement, and measurable value, the Bible makes a radical claim: you matter not because of what you produce, not because of your intelligence or strength or beauty or usefulness. You matter because of whose image you bear. A newborn child has infinite worth. A person with severe intellectual disability has infinite worth. An elderly person in the last stages of dementia has infinite worth. Not because they have achieved something or performed some function, but because they are image-bearers. They carry the mark of the King.

The apostle Peter, writing to early Christians, drew on this ancient understanding and gave it new depth. He called the church "a royal priesthood, a holy nation, God's special possession." Wright draws on the "royal priesthood" language of 1 Peter 2:9 and Exodus 19:6 to describe the restored human vocation in Christ. This language echoes Exodus, where God told Israel at Mount Sinai that they would be "a kingdom of priests and a holy nation." But Peter applied it to all God's people, everywhere. Every believer is a priest. Every believer is royal. This is not because you have been crowned or anointed in a ceremonial sense, but because you have been commissioned. You have been given a vocation that involves both kingship and priesthood.[2]

To be a priest, in biblical terms, is to stand in God's presence and bring the concerns of creation back to him in intercession and praise. To be a king is to represent God's rule in creation, to bring his wisdom and justice into the world. The human vocation is both. We are called to look upward and look outward simultaneously—to worship God and to extend his kingdom. Both directions. Both essential. This is what it means to be made in God's image.

Created for Communion

The vocation to bear God's image is not meant to be lived in isolation. It is relational at its core, woven into the very fabric of what it means to be human. After God created humanity in Genesis, after declaring the work "good," we read something striking: "The Lord God said, 'It is not good for the man to be alone. I will make a helper suitable for him.'" This is the first time in the creation account that God identifies something as "not good." The solitude is not good. Connection is essential.

But the call to communion runs deeper than the creation of a spouse. It touches every dimension of human existence. Humanity was created for communion with God—we see this in the image of God walking in the garden in the cool of the day, conversing with Adam and Eve. Humanity was created for communion with each other—the man and woman are presented not as competitors for resources but as partners in the vocation, a community of image-bearers. And humanity was created for communion with creation itself—not as exploiters, but as stewards and lovers of the world God made.

This relational architecture is not incidental to our humanity. It is constitutive of it. We do not become fully human in isolation. We become human in relationship—with God, with each other, with the world. The person who has everything but is utterly alone is impoverished in the deepest sense. The person who has little but lives in rich community and communion with God possesses something far more valuable than all the world's goods.

The Ten Words that we will explore in this book are shaped by this relational understanding. The first four commandments— about God, idolatry, the Sabbath, and the name of the Lord— order our vertical relationship with God. They establish how we are to love and worship and honor the One whose image we bear. The remaining six commandments—about parents, murder, adultery, theft, false witness, and coveting—order our horizontal relationships with each other. They establish how we are to love and honor and respect the image-bearers around us.

This is why the Ten Words are not a random collection of rules. They reflect the relational structure of human existence itself. To break a commandment is to tear the fabric of communion—to damage your relationship with God or with your neighbor. To keep a commandment is to strengthen it. The Ten Words are, in essence, the grammar of community. They are how communion is both protected and expressed.

Priests in the Temple

To understand the human vocation fully, we need to see creation through a particular lens—one that has been obscured in much modern theology but is absolutely essential to the biblical vision. Genesis does not describe the creation of a universe in the sense of material stuff floating in space. It describes something far more personal: the inauguration of a cosmic temple, God's dwelling place, the place where heaven and earth meet.

The structure of Genesis 1 reflects the ancient temple pattern. In the tabernacle and temple that Israel would later build, there were seven compartments and furniture pieces. In Genesis 1, God works for six days and rests on the seventh. The seventh day—the Sabbath—corresponds to the holy of holies, the innermost sanctuary where God's presence dwelt. What is described in Genesis is the establishment of sacred space. God is creating not just a material world, but his dwelling place.

At the end of the sixth day, God rests. "Thus the heavens and the earth were completed in all their vast array. By the seventh day God had finished the work he had been doing; so on the seventh day he rested from all his work. Then God blessed the seventh day and made it holy, because on it he rested from all the work of creating that he had done." This is not rest that comes from exhaustion. In the ancient worldview, when a god "rested" in a temple, it meant the god took up residence there. God's Sabbath rest is an act of sovereignty and presence. He is saying: I dwell here. I am at home in this creation.

Into this cosmic temple, humanity is placed as priests. The garden is the inner sanctuary, the place closest to God's presence. The human vocation is priestly: to tend the garden, to guard it, to keep it holy. And then to expand outward, to extend the boundaries of God's sacred, ordered presence further and further into creation. Humanity is called to be a bridge between heaven and earth, bringing God's presence and rule into all of creation.[4]

This is why Sabbath is so important—not just as a day off, though it is that. The Sabbath is the heartbeat of the cosmic temple.[3] It is the day of God's presence, the day when the normal work of ordering creation pauses, and creation stops to remember who it belongs to. When Israel rests on the Sabbath, they are not simply taking a break. They are acting out their priestly vocation. They are standing before God in his presence, acknowledging his rule, and joining him in his rest. To keep Sabbath is to be a priest in the cosmic temple.

The importance of this vision cannot be overstated. It means that our ordinary work—tending a garden, building a house, raising children, creating art, serving others—is priestly work. It is work done in God's presence, in his temple. It is work that participates in his creative ordering. But it is work that must be held in balance with rest, with worship, with remembrance. The Sabbath is not an interruption to real work. The Sabbath is real work—the work of being present to God.

The Ten Words as the Grammar of the Vocation

Now we can see how the Ten Words emerge from this understanding of human vocation. They are not arbitrary rules imposed on humanity from outside, rules that restrict freedom and authentic self-expression. They are not the whim of a distant deity who enjoys seeing humans constrained and diminished. They are, rather, the grammar of the vocation. They are the description of what it looks like to live as God's image-bearing, covenant-keeping, priestly people in a world that has been made as God's temple.

"You shall have no other gods before me." The image-bearer worships the God whose image he bears, not any substitute. This is not jealousy on God's part. It is clarity about reality. If you are made in God's image to represent his rule, then to worship another god is to destroy the foundation of your own identity. You cannot serve two masters. The first commandment protects the most basic relationship that makes all other relationships possible.

"You shall not murder." In Genesis 9:6, after the flood, God gives Noah a foundation for law: "Whoever sheds human blood, by humans shall their blood be shed; for in the image of God has God made mankind." To take a human life is to attack the image of God. It is, in a profound sense, an assault on God himself. The commandment against murder flows directly from the dignity of bearing God's image. It protects the sanctuary—not just the building, but the living temple of every human being.

"You shall not steal." To take what belongs to another is to deny their dignity as an image-bearer, to treat them as if their property were more important than their status as a priest in God's temple. Theft is a violation of communion. It is saying: what you have is mine. It is taking something without covenant, without relationship, without honoring the other person's claim over their own life and labor.

"Remember the Sabbath day by keeping it holy." To keep Sabbath is to live out the rhythm of the cosmic temple, to join God in his rest, to acknowledge that creation is his, not ours. To remember the Sabbath is to resist the seduction of endless productivity, to say that human worth is not measured by what we produce. On the Sabbath, we simply be. We join God in his presence. We act out the vocation in its truest form.

"Honor your father and mother." To honor the generations before us is to honor the continuity of the covenant community, the chain of image-bearers through time. It is to recognize that we do not stand alone, that we are part of a story larger than ourselves. The family is the primary school of communion and covenant. To honor father and mother is to practice the fundamental posture of the priestly vocation: respect, humility, recognition of bonds that precede us.

Each commandment could be unpacked this way. Each one is the grammar of the vocation made concrete. Each one describes what happens when the image of God is honored, when communion is protected, when the temple is kept holy. When the Ten Words are kept, the vocation is being lived, sometimes imperfectly, sometimes with struggle, but genuinely. When they are broken, the vocation is being abandoned. The commandments are not constraints on human freedom. They are the pathways to it.

A Dignity That Cannot Be Erased

We live in a time of widespread confusion about human worth. We see it everywhere: in the way we value people based on their productivity or appearance or income or intelligence. In the ways we exploit and dominate those we consider less valuable. In the ways we dehumanize those who disagree with us or threaten us. In the epidemic of loneliness that suggests that connection is being replaced by connectivity, communion replaced by consumption. In a hundred subtle ways, we have forgotten what humans are for.

The deeper problem, though, is not confusion about worth in the abstract. It is abandonment of the vocation itself. Humans were made to be priests in God's temple, to represent his rule, to stand in communion with him and with each other and with all of creation. We were made for work that has meaning, for rest that has rhythm, for love that is mutual and covenantal and deep. And yet the world offers us something else: endless striving, hollow success, the loneliness of achievement. It offers us the mirage of freedom that is actually a kind of slavery—freedom from everything, including the vocation we were made for.

But here is what must be understood, and what will become clearer as we move through the commandments in the chapters to come: the vocation can be abandoned. The image can be rejected.

The temple can be desecrated. But the image itself cannot be erased. Even in the deepest ruin of sin, even in the most profound abandonment of the vocation, the image of God persists. It is not perfectly expressed. It is distorted and diminished. But it is present. This is why restoration makes sense. You can only restore what was real to begin with.

This is the hope that underlies the entire biblical story. The Ten Words are not primarily a diagnosis of what is wrong with humanity—though they are that. They are a summons. They are a call back to what we were made for. They say: You were created for this. This vocation is written into your very being, even if you have forgotten it. You can live this way again. You can return.

The sculptor stands back from his work in the early morning light. The figure is complete now. The chisel is set down. The dust is settling. What stands before him bears the mark of his hands, his vision, his intention. It carries something of his own image—not in the sense that it looks exactly like him, but in the sense that it embodies his thought, his heart, his care. He looks at what he has made, and he knows it was good.

"And God saw everything that he had made, and behold, it was very good."

– (Genesis 1:31)

You were made for glory. Not the false glory of recognition or achievement or dominance. But the true glory of bearing the image of God, of living as his priest in his temple, of standing in communion with him and with each other. It was very good.[5] And in Christ, it will be very good again.

Notes

1. John Walton, *The Lost World of Genesis One: Ancient Cosmology and the Origins Debate* (Downers Grove: IVP Academic, 2009). Walton's "functional ontology" represents a significant reorientation of how evangelicals read Genesis 1, focusing on role and purpose rather than material origins.

2. N.T. Wright, *After You Believe: Why Christian Character Matters* (New York: HarperOne, 2010), 72–80.

3. John Walton, *The Lost World of Adam and Eve: Genesis 2–3 and the Human Origins Debate* (Downers Grove: IVP Academic, 2015), 103–112. The priestly vocation of humanity in the cosmic temple is central to Walton's reading of the garden narrative..

4. Walter Brueggemann, *Sabbath as Resistance: Saying No to the Culture of Now* (Louisville: Westminster John Knox, 2014), 1–10. Brueggemann situates Sabbath within a creation theology that envisions neighborly community as the alternative to empire's competitive individualism

5. N.T. Wright, *Simply Christian: Why Christianity Makes Sense* (New York: HarperOne, 2006), 183–207.

CHAPTER 3

BREAKING THE IMAGE

SIN AND THE COLLAPSE OF HUMANITY

"You have made us for yourself, O Lord, and our heart is restless until it rests in you."

— Augustine of Hippo, Confessions

There is an old mirror in the attic. You find it by accident—reaching for something else, your hand falls on lacquered wood, ornate and heavy. You pull it down, dust clouding in the afternoon light. It is beautiful still. You can see the craftsmanship in the carved frame, the intentionality of its making. Someone loved this mirror once. Someone placed it in a room where it could catch the light and return a true image.

But the glass is cracked. A web of fractures runs from one corner to the other, splintering the reflection into a thousand shards. You stand before it and see yourself—and do not. Your face is there, recognizable. Your features intact. But everything is broken, refracted, doubled, distorted. The image is fragmented. You see yourself multiplied in the cracks, each piece showing something real but nothing whole.

This is the biblical picture of humanity after the fall. The image is not destroyed. God did not smash the mirror and cast it away. The image is not erased. You can still see yourself there, still recognize the contours of what you were made to be. But it is cracked. Everything is fractured. The cracks run deep—not just through your choices but through your desires, not just through what you do but through what you are.

And the tragedy is that you keep using the broken mirror. You keep looking into it, trying to see yourself clearly, trying to find your way. But the cracks multiply. Each time you turn away from the God in whose image you were made, another fracture spreads. Each time you bow before a lesser god, the mirror splinters further. The image cannot lie to you—it is trying desperately to show you the truth. But the truth it shows is the truth of brokenness.

This is what sin does. It breaks the mirror. Not once, but over and over. And the greatest tragedy is not that we break it, but that we keep looking into it, convinced that what we see is what we were made for.

To speak of sin is to speak about something more than just broken rules. It's to speak about broken mirrors—cracks running through the very image we were created to reflect. The biblical vision of humanity is radiant: bearers of God's image, royal priests in a sacred creation, made for worship and communion and life. But that vision has been fractured.

This chapter is not an attempt to catalogue sins or construct a theology of guilt. It is an exploration of how the breaking of the Ten Commandments signals something deeper: a collapse in the architecture of what it means to be human. When the commandments are broken, something more than obedience is lost. Communion is lost. Orientation is lost. The echo of Eden grows faint. And the distortion is not simply vertical (between us and God) but horizontal (between us and each other, between us and creation itself).

The early church father Irenaeus famously said, "The glory of God is a living man" (*Gloria enim Dei vivens homo*).[1] The tragedy of sin, then, is not merely that it incurs divine displeasure, but that it diminishes the very creature who was meant to reflect divine glory. Sin makes us less human.

We will move through each commandment again—but this time, from the vantage point of what its violation does. This is not a descent into despair, but an honest naming of inhumanity. For only what is named can be healed.

Sin as Vocational Failure

The Ten Words are not merely a set of rules to keep us in line. They describe something deeper still. In the vision of N.T. Wright and others, sin is not primarily about breaking rules.[2] It is about the failure of the human vocation. God commissioned humanity as royal priests—to bring His wise, loving rule into creation, and to bring creation's praise back to God. We were made to be priests in the cosmic temple, mediators between heaven and earth, channels through which divine love flows into the world.

Sin is the abandonment of that commission. It is like an ambassador who stops representing the king and starts acting in their own interest. The ambassador is still there. The embassy is still standing. But the connection to the kingdom has been severed. The authority that once flowed through them now flows nowhere. They have authority without representation, power without purpose.

Michael Gorman describes this through the concept of anti-cruciformity.[3] Sin is the inversion of the self-giving love that defines God's own character. Where Christ empties Himself for others (Philippians 2:5-8—the kenotic pattern), sin fills itself at others' expense. The gravitational pull of sin is always inward. Augustine called it *incurvatus in se*, "the soul curved in on itself." Luther picked up this language. The soul curved inward. The heart folded in on itself. Sin curves us away from God and away from neighbor, until all that remains is the small, cramped universe of the self.

John Walton speaks of the cosmic temple imagery.[4] When the priests abandon the temple, the temple is not destroyed. But its function is disrupted. The garden, meant to be a place where heaven and earth overlap, becomes a place of exile. The sacred geography of creation is disordered. The priests stop speaking to God on behalf of creation. Creation stops hearing from God through human mediation. The conversation is broken.

Reflections on the Commandments

You shall have no other gods before me. (Exodus 20:3)

At the center of all things stands a simple, shattering truth: there is one God, and we are not Him. This Word unmasks our divided loyalties. It confronts every empire, every idol, every false self we build. To have no other gods is not only a command; it is the declaration of reality itself: the universe has a center, and it is not us. Our hearts, restless and wandering, crave lesser loves. We enthrone success, comfort, nation, pleasure. We bow before shadows and wonder why we are still afraid. The First Word calls us home to singularity. To worship the living God alone is to find at last a center strong enough to bear the weight of existence.

You shall not make for yourself an idol. (Exodus 20:4)

Idolatry is not merely a failure of piety; it is a failure of imagination. To fashion an idol is to reduce the infinite to the manageable, to domesticate mystery into control. Every idol is a shrunken god—one we can carry in our pocket, consult on our terms, and dismiss when convenient. But such a god cannot save. It can only mirror our own desires back at us, endlessly amplified. Ellen Davis writes: "Idolatry is not only the worship of false gods; it is the worship of false selves."[5] The sin of idolatry distorts not only our theology but our identity.

You shall not take the name of the Lord your God in vain. (Exodus 20:7)

The name of God is not just a label; it is a window into reality. In Hebrew, the word for "vain" (*shav'*) suggests falsehood and emptiness. To take God's name in vain is to speak of ultimate reality as if it were trivial—to use the name of the Creator of all things as punctuation, as leverage, as a branding tool. This commandment guards the integrity of language itself. When God's name is hollowed out, all language suffers. Truth becomes negotiable. Words become weapons.

Remember the Sabbath day and keep it holy. (Exodus 20:8)

The breaking of Sabbath is the breaking of creaturely identity. We forget that we are creatures. We forget that the world does not run on our energy. We forget that rest is not laziness but trust—trust that the God who made the world can keep it running while we sleep. Abraham Heschel called the Sabbath "a sanctuary in time."[6] When we demolish that sanctuary, we are left with the ruins of our own exhaustion, convinced that our worth is measured in output.

Honor your father and your mother. (Exodus 20:12)

To dishonor the generations that preceded us is to sever ourselves from the story that made us. It is to pretend that we arrived without debt, without inheritance, without the weight of others' love. It is also to declare that the future owes us nothing—for what we do to the past, the young will do to us. Covenant life is intergenerational. Dishonor breaks the chain.

You shall not murder. (Exodus 20:13)

To murder is to declare that another human being does not matter —that their life, their voice, their irreplaceable particularity can be cancelled. The Hebrew ratsach refers to unlawful killing, but the spirit of the commandment extends further: to dehumanize, to reduce, to erase. Every act of violence against a person is an act of violence against God, who made that person in His image. "Whoever sheds the blood of man, by man shall his blood be shed, for God made man in his own image" (Genesis 9:6).

You shall not commit adultery. (Exodus 20:14)

Adultery fractures covenant. It tears at the sacred binding of trust —the kind of trust that says "I choose you, and I will keep choosing you." But the damage runs deeper than broken marriages. Adultery teaches the soul that promises are optional, that desire is its own law, that commitment is conditional on satisfaction. It seeds distrust into the most intimate spaces of human life.

You shall not steal. (Exodus 20:15)

Theft is a declaration that what belongs to another can be taken—that their labor, their dignity, their property are not truly theirs. But theft is not only about possessions. We steal time, credit, reputation, opportunity. Every act of theft communicates to the person stolen from: you do not fully belong to yourself. Your life is available for my convenience. This is the logic of empire dressed in ordinary clothes.

You shall not bear false witness against your neighbor. (Exodus 20:16)

False witness destroys community at its root. Community depends on shared language, on the trust that words mean what they say. When false witness enters, it poisons the well. Not just for the one falsely accused—but for everyone. It teaches people to doubt, to suspect, to arm themselves against the spoken word. Falsehood weaponizes language and makes trust impossible.

You shall not covet. (Exodus 20:17)

The Tenth Word turns the searchlight inward. It exposes not what we do but what we want. Coveting is the desire that has turned from gratitude toward grasping—that looks at another person's life and feels not celebration but resentment. Coveting says: what they have should be mine. It poisons the heart before it poisons behavior. It is the seedbed of almost every other sin.

The Shape of Inhumanity

Each commandment, when broken, reveals not just a rule violated but a reflection shattered. Together, they trace the contours of inhumanity—a world where God is replaced by idols, rest is replaced by exhaustion, truth is replaced by manipulation, love is replaced by exploitation.

The commandments do not merely describe moral failure. They describe ontological collapse—the unraveling of what it means to be fully human. When we read them as a negative, we see the diagnosis. And diagnosis is the beginning of healing.

Sin is not only the breaking of divine law, but the breaking of divine communion. — Thomas F. Torrance[7]

This is why the Ten Words matter—not as relics of ancient morality, but as mirrors held up to a broken world, showing us the shape of what we have lost, and whispering that there is still a way home.

The Mercy Within the Diagnosis

The diagnosis is not the end. The very act of naming sin—of saying "this is not what you were made for"—is itself an act of grace. To diagnose is to assume that health is possible. You don't diagnose a stone. You don't diagnose what is irredeemably broken. The very fact that Scripture tells us what sin is assumes that we can turn from it. The very fact that God gave us the Ten Words assumes that we can hear them, understand them, and choose another way.

Michael Gorman reminds us that the cruciform God does not stand at a distance from human brokenness. He enters it. The cross is the place where the depth of human sin and the depth of divine love meet—and divine love wins.[8] The diagnosis of inhumanity is only devastating if there is no doctor. But there is.

The Ten Words, read in light of Christ, are not ultimately a verdict. They are a vocation renewed. Each word that named our failure is also, in Christ, a promise of restoration. "You shall have no other gods" becomes, in Christ, "you will find in me the only God you need." "You shall not murder" becomes, in Christ, "I will give you a heart that loves even its enemies." "You shall not covet" becomes, in Christ, "I will satisfy the deepest longings of your heart."

We are not well. But we are not abandoned. And the One who made us knows the way home.

Notes

1. Irenaeus of Lyon, *Against Heresies*, 4.20.7. The phrase "Gloria enim Dei vivens homo" has been much discussed; its full context suggests that the glory of God is most visible in humanity fully alive in relationship with God.

2. N.T. Wright, *The Day the Revolution Began: Reconsidering the Meaning of Jesus's Crucifixion* (New York: HarperOne, 2016), 74–92.

3. Michael Gorman, *Cruciformity: Paul's Narrative Spirituality of the Cross* (Grand Rapids: Eerdmans, 2001), 4–15. Gorman's term "cruciformity" describes the shape of Paul's spirituality—always conformed to the pattern of Christ's death and resurrection.

4. John Walton, *The Lost World of Adam and Eve: Genesis 2–3 and the Human Origins Debate* (Downers Grove: IVP Academic, 2015), 145–155.

5. Ellen F. Davis, *Proverbs, Ecclesiastes, and the Song of Songs* (Westminster John Knox, 2000), 20. Davis's observation about idolatry and false selfhood reflects broader themes in her approach to Old Testament ethics.

6. Abraham Heschel, *The Sabbath: Its Meaning for Modern Man* (New York: Farrar, Straus and Giroux, 1951), 8.

7. .Thomas F. Torrance, *The Mediation of Christ* (Edinburgh: T&T Clark, 1992), 39.

8. Michael Gorman, *Inhabiting the Cruciform God: Kenosis, Justification, and Theosis in Paul's Narrative Soteriology* (Grand Rapids: Eerdmans, 2009), 9–39.

CHAPTER 4

EGYPT, EMPIRE, AND INHUMANITY

"When the rulers of the earth forget justice, the Lord still remembers." — Psalm 9:17-18 (paraphrased)

The brickyard wakes before dawn. There is no mercy in the Nile mud—it demands, and demands early. The overseer's whistle pierces the darkness, a sound the Hebrew man has learned to hate with the precision of a surgeon's blade. He is already awake, has been awake for hours, his body having forgotten the difference between sleep and waking some seasons ago. The fear wakes him before the whistle does.

He rises from the mat—if the torn fabric in the corner can be called a mat—and feels the weight of the straw in his fingernails, the ache in his knees that no amount of water will wash away. His hands are cracked, bled white at the edges, caked with the dust of yesterday's quota and the day before and the day before that. He doesn't know how long he has been here. Years have lost their names.

The smell of the Nile is thick in the air—mud and water and something ancient, something that doesn't change even as everything else does. Around him, others are stirring. Children, thin-limbed and hollow-eyed. Women whose backs are bent not from age but from years of carrying. Men like him, already exhausted before the day begins, muscles remembering labor that hasn't yet come.

A child cries somewhere—hunger, cold, fear, it doesn't matter which. The overseer's footsteps grow closer. The man can hear them now, the deliberate pace of someone who owns the ground they walk on. In Egypt, the ground owns you.

He thinks, for a moment, of a song. His grandmother used to sing it, back when his grandmother was alive, back when there were grandmothers and not just workers. Something about stars. Something about promises. A man named Abraham—was that his name?—and a voice that said, "I will make of you a great nation." The words are slipping away now, like water through fingers. In Egypt, songs die quickly. First the melody goes, then the words, then the memory that there was ever singing at all.

The overseer's shadow falls across the entrance to the barracks. Another day is beginning. The quota will not shrink. The mercy will not come. The sky is still dark, but the Nile mud doesn't care. It is waiting. It is always waiting.

This is the world into which the Ten Words were spoken. Not into a library or a sanctuary. Not into the minds of philosophers or the courts of the powerful. Into a brickyard. Into the lungs and bones of people who had forgotten what it felt like not to be afraid.

The Ten Commandments were not given in a vacuum. They were not whispered into an untouched paradise or handed down to a tranquil people meditating by rivers. They were spoken to a community that had just escaped the world's most powerful empire. They were given to former slaves.

Israel met God in the wilderness, but they carried Egypt in their bones. The commandments, then, were not merely instructions; they were a re-humanizing declaration. They were spoken not only to guide Israel's future but to counter their past—to offer an entirely different imagination of what human community could look like.

In this chapter, we will explore the world of empire that formed the backdrop for the commandments. We will look not only at the historical conditions of Egypt, but at the broader political-theological phenomenon of empire—what it does to persons, what it does to communities, and why the Ten Words stand in such sharp contrast to its logic. We will trace the pattern of Pharaoh's world from ancient Egypt through history to our own time.

To understand the depth of the Decalogue, we must understand the world it was meant to contrast. And to understand what it means to be human, we must first name what has made humanity a thing to be used.

Pharaoh's World — Egypt as a Machine of Dehumanization

To speak of Egypt in the Exodus tradition is to speak of systemic inhumanity. It is not simply the story of one cruel ruler, but of an entire regime organized around exploitation. The book of Exodus introduces us to a Pharaoh "who did not know Joseph" (Exod. 1:8)—a ruler who has severed himself from the memory of covenant, from the story of divine generosity that made Egypt prosperous through Israel's presence. Now the Israelites are threats to be managed.

What we find is a portrait of oppression that is at once ancient and startlingly modern: forced labor, surveillance, infanticide, and dehumanization through mass productivity. The Hebrews are reduced to labor units. Their value is measured in bricks. Their future is controlled by fear.

The empire is not interested in covenant. It does not care for the sanctity of rest or the dignity of persons. It seeks only growth. And when that growth is threatened, it doubles down. Pharaoh responds to Moses's request for a three-day religious observance not with dialogue, but with increased quotas (Exod. 5:7–19). Liberation is inconceivable within the empire's imagination.

In Egypt, there is no Sabbath. No gift. No release. Only production. And when the system begins to fail, it blames the most vulnerable.

The dehumanization of empire is not merely physical; it is imaginative. It reshapes what people believe is possible. After years of slavery, even freedom can sound terrifying. When faced with scarcity in the wilderness, Israel's instinct was to long for Egypt — where, despite the chains, at least there were "pots of meat" (Exod. 16:3). Empire is not just a political system; it is a form of soul-formation. It teaches people to want small things.

The Decalogue as an Anti-Imperial Manifesto

The Ten Commandments do not simply oppose Egypt's tyranny in abstract moral terms—they unmask it, counter it, and call forth a new society built on a radically different imagination.

Where Egypt said, "Work without rest," the fourth commandment says, "Remember the Sabbath." Where Pharaoh's economy commodified human labor, the Decalogue restores dignity to the laborer. The Sabbath is not just a religious observance; it is a political statement. It announces that human beings are not defined by their productivity. That no system has the right to claim all of a person's time.

Likewise, where Egypt devalued life—slaughtering infants, crushing spirits—the commandments reassert the sacredness of each person. "You shall not murder," "You shall not steal," "You shall not bear false witness" — each of these words stands against the empire's logic of exploitation.

Where Egypt taught that truth is whatever Pharaoh declares it to be, the Ninth Word insists on truthful speech. Where Pharaoh cultivated endless desire for more, the Tenth Word confronts covetousness at its root.

The Decalogue is not a polite supplement to imperial culture. It is its antithesis. It calls into existence an alternative community— one where the dignity of every person is protected, where rest is holy, where truth binds even the powerful, and where desire is ordered toward the neighbor's good rather than the neighbor's destruction.

Empire Beyond Egypt

Pharaoh's Egypt was not unique. The pattern repeats throughout history — the same logic, different costumes. The book of

Revelation, written during Roman imperial rule, uses the same imagery: Babylon as the empire that demands total loyalty, corrupts imagination, and trades in human lives (Rev. 18:13).

Walter Brueggemann has mapped this pattern with prophetic clarity[1]. He identifies a "royal consciousness" — a dominant cultural imagination that presents the current order as natural, inevitable, and permanent. Royal consciousness numbs people to the possibility of change. It domesticates grief and suppresses hope. It presents the empire's categories as the only categories.

The prophetic tradition — which gave us the Decalogue — stands against this. The prophets refused to accept the empire's definitions. They remembered a different world. They dared to imagine a world where justice rolled down like waters (Amos 5:24), where the hungry were fed and the proud scattered (Luke 1:51-53), where the first would be last.

From Babylon to Rome to the modern nation-state, the logic of empire persists. What changes is its technology. What remains is its hunger.

Prophetic Consciousness and Imperial Consciousness

Brueggemann's key insight in *The Prophetic Imagination* is that there are two competing "imaginaries" at war in every age. The royal or imperial consciousness—which numbs grief, domesticates hope, and presents the current order as eternal and unchangeable. And the prophetic consciousness—which permits grief by naming the pain the empire denies, energizes hope by imagining a world the empire says is impossible, and calls the community to live by a different script.[2]

The Ten Words are a prophetic document. They begin not with rules but with memory. "I am the LORD your God, who brought you out of Egypt, out of the house of slavery" (Exod. 20:2). This preamble is the most important verse in the Decalogue. It names the alternative memory—the God who acts on behalf of the enslaved against the empire. Every commandment that follows grows from this alternative memory. This is not top-down law imposed from above; this is liberation speaking.

To practice the Ten Words is to practice prophetic consciousness. To keep Sabbath is to remember that the world is held by God, not by Pharaoh. To tell the truth is to refuse the empire's management of reality. To honor parents is to keep covenant memory alive against the empire's amnesia. To not covet is to resist the endless wanting that empire cultivates. Each commandment is a conscious act of resistance to the royal imagination and a yes to a different way of being human.

This is why the Decalogue could not have been written in a palace or a center of power. It had to be spoken from the wilderness—the place where imperial logic has no grip, where survival is daily and real, where people are desperate enough to imagine that another world is possible. The prophetic imagination is born in the place the empire has abandoned, and from there it speaks words that will echo through the ages.

Living Against Empire — The Decalogue for Today

We do not need to look far to find Pharaoh's logic at work today. It lives in economic systems that demand endless growth at human cost. It lives in media ecosystems that commodify attention. It lives in political movements that scapegoat the vulnerable. It lives in corporate cultures that value output over persons.

The Decalogue, spoken to former slaves, is still spoken to those living under modern forms of empire. It says: you are more than what you produce. Your worth is not determined by your market value. Rest is not a luxury — it is a right inscribed in the rhythm of creation. Truth matters. Dignity matters. The neighbor matters.

This is not a call to withdraw from the world but to live within it differently — as witnesses to a different order, a different imagination, a different King.

The Long Exodus and the Human Vocation

The story of the Exodus is not finished. N.T. Wright has argued powerfully that the Exodus functions as the paradigmatic story of redemption — the pattern that the New Testament sees fulfilled and enlarged in Christ's death and resurrection. The "new Exodus" theme runs from Isaiah through Paul: the ultimate liberation is not from Egypt but from sin and death itself.[3]

The divine warrior motif—God fighting against empire on behalf of the oppressed—runs through the Exodus narrative with prophetic power.[4] Each plague is not a random act of cosmic force but a targeted assault on the gods of Egypt. The plagues deconstruct the very theological foundation of the empire. The frogs, the locust, the darkness—each plague corresponds to an Egyptian deity, demonstrating that the gods Pharaoh trusts are powerless. God is not merely freeing a people; He is dismantling an entire religious and political order. The victory at the Red Sea is a holy war—the divine warrior fighting for His people against the military power of the world's greatest empire.

In the New Testament, this same pattern resurfaces with cosmic significance. The cross and resurrection are the ultimate Exodus event. Jesus goes into the Egypt of sin and death—bearing the curse, descending into darkness—and emerges victorious on Easter morning, leading His people out of bondage. The giving of the Spirit at Pentecost is the new Sinai—the law now written on hearts of flesh, not on stone. The church becomes the new covenant community formed by the new Exodus. Paul makes this explicit: "He has rescued us from the domain of darkness and transferred us into the kingdom of his beloved Son" (Col. 1:13)—Exodus language, now applied to the cosmic liberation achieved in Christ.[5]

The Ten Words, given at Sinai after the first Exodus, are now written on hearts by the Spirit after the greater Exodus of the cross. Jeremiah anticipated this: "I will put my law within them, and I will write it on their hearts; and I will be their God, and they shall be my people" (Jer. 31:33). Ezekiel deepened the vision: "I will give you a new heart and put a new spirit within you; and I will remove the heart of stone from your flesh and give you a heart of flesh" (Ezek. 36:26). This is no longer external law but internal transformation. The Ten Words are no longer inscribed on tablets carried by a priest but alive in the very being of God's people.

The human vocation—distorted by sin, crushed by empire, seemingly lost forever—is being restored. The long Exodus continues. It is a journey that began in Egypt and has not ended. Every act of resistance to dehumanization, every practice of Sabbath rest, every truth spoken against falsehood, every dignity honored in a world that commodifies persons, every instance of forgiveness, every choice to love the neighbor instead of covet what the neighbor has—these are not mere moral gestures. They are steps on the journey home. They are the Ten Words spoken into our flesh, reminding us who we were made to be.

Notes

1. Walter Brueggemann, *The Prophetic Imagination*, 2nd ed. (Minneapolis: Fortress Press, 2001), 1–19.

2. Walter Brueggemann, *Theology of the Old Testament: Testimony, Dispute, Advocacy* (Minneapolis: Fortress Press, 1997), 175–182. Brueggemann's treatment of the Exodus as Israel's foundational "counter-testimony" to the claims of empire.

3. N.T. Wright, *The Day the Revolution Began: Reconsidering the Meaning of Jesus's Crucifixion* (New York: HarperOne, 2016), 84–102. Wright's argument that the cross is best understood as the climactic Exodus event.

4. Tremper Longman III and Daniel G. Reid, *God Is a Warrior* (Grand Rapids: Zondervan, 1995), 28–45.

5. N.T. Wright, *Paul and the Faithfulness of God* (Minneapolis: Fortress Press, 2013), 408–477. The new Exodus in Pauline theology.

CHAPTER 5

COVENANT AND THE RECOVERY OF THE HUMAN HEART

"I will give you a new heart, and a new spirit I will put within you." — Ezekiel 36:26

A Wedding in a Small Country Church

The sanctuary is modest, spare. Two candles flicker on the altar. There is no elaborate processional, no string quartet, no cascade of flowers. Just two people standing before witnesses — family mostly, a handful of friends — in a small country church where generations have made promises before God.

He is nervous. You can see it in the way his hands tremble as he holds hers. She looks up at him, and her eyes are bright with tears not yet shed. The pastor reads from 1 Corinthians 13: "Love is patient, love is kind." Ordinary words, words spoken at ten thousand weddings, and yet in this moment they carry the weight of a vow about to be made.

"For better, for worse," she says, and her voice breaks slightly on the words.

"For richer, for poorer," he continues.

"In sickness and in health," they say together, hands joined so tightly the knuckles whiten.

"Until death do us part."

The ring goes on. A simple band of gold, catching the light as it slides onto her finger. When the pastor pronounces them bound together, something shifts in the room. The air itself feels different. He leans forward and kisses her. The witnesses applaud. But both of them know — something has changed. Irreversibly. Beautifully. They are no longer two separate people making separate choices. They are bound. Covenanted. Free to choose each other because they have, in this moment, chosen to give away the absolute freedom of choosing alone.

God did this. At Sinai, with a people freshly freed from chains, amid thunder and cloud and the trembling of a mountain, God made a wedding. He bound himself to them before He gave them commandments. Obligation followed relationship. Law followed love. This is the sequence that changes everything.

Covenant as the Context for the Commandments

At Sinai, God does not begin with law; God begins with relationship. This covenantal structure is what distinguishes the Ten Commandments from mere legal codes of the ancient Near East. Though other ancient law codes exist — the Code of Hammurabi, the Laws of Eshnunna — they do not begin with redemption. They begin with power. The God of Israel begins differently: with a story of deliverance.

As Michael Horton observes, "The Decalogue presupposes a redeemed community in covenant with their God, not individuals striving for merit."[1] The commandments are not hurdles to win God's favor; they are the contours of a life lived in God's family.

They describe the shape of grateful response, not the conditions for divine acceptance.

Covenant is God's answer to empire. Where Pharaoh saw slaves to exploit, Yahweh sees children to cherish. Where empire demands production, covenant invites presence. Where empire erases faces, covenant calls them by name.

The commandments, then, are not impersonal dictates but covenantal terms—the house rules of a family bound together by divine love.

This relational setting also explains the order of the commandments. They flow outward from love of God to love of neighbor (cf. Matt. 22:37–40). Covenant life is not segmented into religious and social spheres — it is seamlessly woven together.

Thus, to honor God rightly is to honor the neighbor rightly. To misuse God's name is to mistreat human names. To desecrate Sabbath time is to desecrate the rhythms that sustain communities. Covenant is integrative.

It is also fragile. The biblical narrative shows that covenant can be broken—not because God is unfaithful, but because the human heart is.

The Human Heart and the Challenge of Covenant Faithfulness

Israel's history is, in many ways, the history of covenant made and covenant betrayed. No sooner is the covenant established than it is endangered. As Moses lingers on the mountain receiving the commandments, the people below are already melting down their gold to build a calf (Exod. 32). The ink is barely dry on the covenant scroll, and the heart has already wandered.

This is not simply Israel's problem. It is the human problem. The prophet Jeremiah, writing centuries later, diagnoses the crisis: "The heart is deceitful above all things, and desperately sick; who can understand it?" (Jer. 17:9). The commandments reveal the shape of the good life — but they cannot by themselves reform the heart that keeps running away from it.

This is where the prophetic tradition begins to anticipate something more — a covenant renewal that reaches deeper than law can reach. Ezekiel envisions a day when God himself will perform surgery on the human heart: "I will remove the heart of stone from your flesh and give you a heart of flesh. And I will put my Spirit within you, and cause you to walk in my statutes" (Ezek. 36:26-27). The Ten Words, written on stone, will one day be written on living hearts.

This is not a dismissal of the commandments but their fulfillment. The goal was never mere external compliance. The goal was always a people whose hearts had been so shaped by God's grace that obedience would become joy.

Jesus and the Fulfillment of Covenant

Jesus stands at the center of the covenant story. He does not come to discard the commandments but to fulfill them — to press them deeper, to embody them completely, and ultimately to write them on human hearts through the Spirit he sends.

In the Sermon on the Mount, Jesus does not abolish the law — he radicalizes it. "You have heard that it was said to those of old, 'You shall not murder'... But I say to you that everyone who is angry with his brother will be liable to judgment" (Matt. 5:21-22). Jesus reaches past behavior to the root — the imagination, the desire, the orientation of the whole person. He is not making the law harder; he is revealing what the law was always about.

Jesus fulfills covenant not as a legal transaction but as an act of love. He keeps every commandment his people could not keep. He bears the covenant curse on their behalf (Gal. 3:13). And in his resurrection, he inaugurates the new covenant promised by Jeremiah and Ezekiel — a covenant not written on stone but on hearts, not enforced by external pressure but empowered by the Spirit.

Covenant Renewal and the Church's Vocation

The church is called to be a covenant community — a people whose shared life embodies the alternative imagination of the Decalogue in the midst of empire. This is not triumphalism; it is witness. It is saying with our lives: we have been brought out of slavery, and we live by different rhythms.

The practices of covenant community are the practices of the Ten Words: gathered worship (no other gods), honest speech (no false witness), care for the vulnerable (no theft, no murder), Sabbath rhythms of rest and feasting, the honoring of the generations. These are not merely religious duties. They are political and theological acts. They say: there is another King. There is another way to be human.

Covenant as the Plan to Put the World Right

The covenant with Israel is not an ethnic preference or a religious arrangement — it is God's chosen means of addressing the problem of evil and restoring creation. Scripture presents a grand narrative arc: Genesis 1 opens with creation declared good, humanity made in God's image. Genesis 3 introduces sin — the fracture of relationship between God and humanity, and between humans themselves. By Genesis 11, the fracture has widened into the catastrophe of empire: the Tower of Babel, where humanity gathers to build glory for itself, to establish power through centralized control.

Into this chaos, God speaks a word of election. He calls one man, Abraham, and makes a covenant: "In you all the families of the earth shall be blessed" (Gen. 12:3). This is God's response to the human failure documented in Genesis 1–11. God does not respond with obliteration but with purpose. He chooses Israel to be the means through which God's blessing is extended to all humanity.[2]

The covenant is missional from the beginning. Israel's calling is not to be favored for its own sake but to be the community through whom God's purposes for all humanity are advanced. The Ten Words are the covenant's operating principle. They do not just govern Israel's internal life — they shape Israel into a community that, by its very way of living, witnesses to the nations what truly human life looks like. When Israel lives by the Decalogue, the nations see an alternative to empire. When Israel fails — and it often does — the witness is obscured.

This is the background to the new covenant in Christ. Jesus, as the true Israel, fulfills the covenant that Israel could not. He lives the Ten Words perfectly. He witnesses to the nations perfectly. And he extends the covenant to all people through faith — so that "in Christ Jesus" all people can become "Abraham's offspring, heirs according to promise" (Gal. 3:28-29). The goal of God, from the beginning, is not just to have one covenant people but to have a covenant people spanning all nations, united in Christ.[3]

Covenant Faithfulness and the Pattern of the Cross

What is the shape of covenant faithfulness? Look at God's own covenant commitment. God does not covenant with Israel because they are powerful or deserving. Moses reminds Israel: "It was not because you were more in number than any other people that the LORD set his love on you... but it is because the LORD loves you" (Deut. 7:7). God chooses them freely, lavishly, at cost to himself.

This pattern — free, undeserved, self-giving love — is what Paul sees crystallized at the cross. "God shows his love for us in that while we were still sinners, Christ died for us" (Rom. 5:8). The cross is the covenant in its most concentrated form. The commandments, which describe the shape of covenant life, find their source and center in the One who kept covenant love all the way to death.

To live the Ten Words, then, is not just to follow rules. It is to participate in the pattern of the cross — to love freely, to give ourselves away, to refuse the imperial logic of self-preservation at others' expense. It is to be cruciform: shaped by the cross, bearing witness to the crucified and risen Lord. When we keep covenant in this way — when we do not steal because we trust God's provision, when we do not kill because we have learned the infinite worth of the image-bearer, when we rest on the Sabbath because we believe that the world runs on grace, not our productivity — we are saying yes to a pattern that the cross has revealed and authorized. We are joining our lives to the movement of God's own self-giving love.[4]

Covenant, Hope, and the Final Restoration

The covenant story is not finished. The new covenant inaugurated in Christ will find its final expression in the new creation — a world where the signs of God's presence are fully legible, where every human being fully reflects the divine image, where covenant communion is complete.

John's vision of the new Jerusalem is a covenantal vision: "They will be his people, and God himself will be with them as their God" (Rev. 21:3) — the covenant formula, spoken at last in its fullness. The Ten Words, written on stone at Sinai, written on hearts by the Spirit, will one day be unnecessary because they will be inseparable from who we are.

Until that day, we live as covenant people in a broken world — holding the words, practicing the rhythms, and keeping our eyes fixed on the One who is faithful when we are not.[5]

Notes

1. Michael Horton, *The Christian Faith: A Systematic Theology for Pilgrims on the Way* (Grand Rapids: Zondervan, 2011), 549. Horton's point is that the Decalogue is given to a people already redeemed, not as a means of earning redemption.

2. N.T. Wright, *The New Testament and the People of God* (Minneapolis: Fortress Press, 1992), 268–279.

3. N.T. Wright, *Paul and the Faithfulness of God* (Minneapolis: Fortress Press, 2013), 775–780. Wright's reading of Galatians 3 and the covenant with Abraham as the framework for understanding justification.

4. Michael Gorman, *Cruciformity: Paul's Narrative Spirituality of the Cross* (Grand Rapids: Eerdmans, 2001), 76–100. Gorman's identification of the kenotic pattern (Phil. 2:5-11) as the grammar of both God's character and authentic Christian discipleship.

5. Walter Brueggemann, *The Covenanted Self: Explorations in Law and Covenant* (Minneapolis: Fortress Press, 1999), 1–16. Brueggemann situates covenant faithfulness within the alternative imagination of Israel's prophetic tradition.

Chapter 6

Inhumanity Named

"Sin is not only the breaking of divine law, but the breaking of divine communion." — Thomas F. Torrance[1]

The Doctor's Diagnosis

The medical office is quiet in that particular way of waiting rooms. Soft lighting, neutral walls, the hum of recirculated air. A patient sits on the edge of the examination table while the doctor clicks on the lightbox. X-rays bloom into view—a chest cavity rendered in shadow and silver, the body made visible, made legible to trained eyes.

The doctor points to a hairline fracture running through the bone. "There," she says. Not harshly. Not with alarm. Just: here is what is true.

The patient looks. What the doctor sees—the break, the misalignment—reads to the untrained eye only as light and shadow, an anomaly in the gray.

"Is it bad?" the patient asks, as if the question might change what is there.

"It's what it is," the doctor says. "The good news is, now we know. And now we can treat it."

Diagnosis is not the enemy of healing. Diagnosis is healing's beginning.

The Ten Words function like those X-rays. They reveal fractures most of us have learned to live around without recognizing. Not to condemn us. Not to shame us. But to say: here is what is true. We have learned to walk crooked, to organize our lives around the breaks we no longer notice. And once we see them—really see them—recovery becomes possible. The signs point not only to what we have become, but to what we can become again.

There's something about the Ten Commandments that resists being tamed. Even when framed in polished mahogany on a church wall or recited with polite cadence from a pulpit, their voice still echoes with an elemental weight. They don't just ask to be heard—they demand it. Not because they are loud in the way of thunderclaps, but because they go deep into the foundation of what it means to be alive.

At first glance, this may seem like an overstatement. The commandments are, after all, just ten terse lines of moral instruction. But the deeper you sit with them, the more you begin to notice their underlying architecture. They are not arbitrary laws tossed down from heaven like divine ultimatums. They are—as we have been discovering together—signs. Signs pointing to the deep structure of reality as God intended it.

We have spent five chapters building toward this moment. We have seen that the Ten Words are signs—not arbitrary rules, but markers pointing to the deep structure of reality as God designed it. We have seen that humanity was designed as image-bearers, priests in God's cosmic temple, called to worship, rest, and neighborly community. We have seen how sin distorted the image, how empire institutionalized the distortion, and how covenant held out the hope of recovery.

Now we read the signs in their negative. Not what they point toward when honored—but what the world looks like when they are broken. Each commandment, violated, names a specific form of inhumanity. Together, they map the territory of the broken human condition. This is not pessimism. It is precision. The surgeon needs to know where the cancer is before the healing can begin.

What happens when these commandments are not kept? More specifically, what kind of world takes shape when each of these ten core commitments is broken, whether by individuals or by societies? It is that darker mirror we hold up in this chapter. By examining what each commandment assumes and affirms about human flourishing, we begin to see the inverse: the shape of inhumanity, the contours of a world unmade. The commandments do not only point us toward a moral life; they warn us against a dehumanized one.

The goal here is not to moralize, nor to weaponize Scripture as a bludgeon against others. It is to pause and listen to what the commandments are still trying to tell us—not only about God's holiness, but about our own fragile vocation as image-bearers. What we will discover is that these ancient words are a mirror— and in their reflection, we see both who we have been and who we were meant to be.

So let us begin again at the beginning. Not with doctrine or dogma, but with something more immediate: the voice that calls from the mountain, the echo that still asks, in every generation, "What kind of humans will you be?"

The Commandments Revisited

"You shall have no other gods before me" (Exod. 20:3).

This commandment declares that human beings are worshipping creatures. To place anything other than the living God at the center of one's life is to begin the slow, subtle descent into misalignment. Idolatry doesn't just change the object of devotion —it warps the devotee. It is the original misdirection. Every other form of inhumanity flows downstream from this one, the displacement of God by lesser things. When God is not God, everything else becomes distorted.

"You shall not make for yourself an idol" (Exod. 20:4).

To make an idol is to render God small and manageable. But the biblical God is not containable. The danger of idolatry is not simply in the carving of wood or stone, but in the construction of theology that confirms all our biases and sanctifies our desires. Ellen Davis writes, "Idolatry is not only the worship of false gods; it is the worship of false selves[2]." This is the second breaking of the sign: we not only replace God with lesser things, we replace ourselves with lesser versions of who we were made to be.

"You shall not take the name of the Lord your God in vain" (Exod. 20:7).

The name of God carries weight—it was never meant to be used lightly or manipulatively. In Hebrew, the word for "vain" (שָׁוְא, shav') also suggests falsehood or emptiness. The commandment warns against speaking of God in ways that are hollow, performative, or self-serving. When God's name is emptied of meaning, all meaning empties. The capacity for truthful speech—the foundation of covenant community—begins to erode. We become people who use words to manage reality rather than to describe it.

"Remember the Sabbath day and keep it holy" (Exod. 20:8).

This commandment pushes against our obsession with productivity. It offers not just rest, but resistance—against the empires of endless work and self-justification. Abraham Heschel famously described the Sabbath as "a sanctuary in time."[3] Without Sabbath, we risk forgetting that we are creatures, not gods. We risk confusing our value with our output. The breaking of Sabbath is the breaking of creaturely identity. Exhaustion becomes normal. Overextension becomes virtue. And the quiet, holy recognition that we are held by One greater than ourselves— that recognition slowly fades.

"Honor your father and your mother" (Exod. 20:12).

This command roots us in generational identity. It's not about idealizing the past, but recognizing the continuity of covenant life. When we dishonor our parents, we are not merely breaking a social norm—we are severing ourselves from the story that shaped us. We become orphans of memory. And a people without memory is a people who can be shaped by any story, however false, however dangerous.

"You shall not murder" (Exod. 20:13).

This is not just a prohibition against violence; it is a reverent affirmation of life. In Hebrew, the term is רָצַח (*ratsach*), which refers specifically to unlawful killing. To murder is to attack the image of God in another, and to scar the sacred bond of human dignity. As Genesis 9:6 puts it, to shed human blood is to assault God himself. Murder is the ultimate act of dehumanization—the declaration that this life, this image-bearer, does not matter.

"You shall not commit adultery" (Exod. 20:14).

Adultery tears at the fabric of covenant. It's not only about sex; it's about trust, truth, and the stability of families and communities. It undermines the very idea that promises can be kept and honored. More fundamentally, adultery breaks the covenantal imagination—it says that commitment is conditional, that pledged love is provisional, that the self's desires ultimately override the neighbor's dignity.

"You shall not steal" (Exod. 20:15).

To steal is to deny another's dignity. It treats what is theirs as if it can be taken without regard for their humanity. This applies to more than possessions: theft of time, of credit, of opportunity—each violates covenantal justice. Theft, at its root, is the declaration that I matter and you don't—that your image-bearing life and the fruit of your labor are merely resources for my advancement.

"You shall not bear false witness against your neighbor" (Exod. 20:16).

Falsehood undermines truth, and truth is the foundation of justice. Lying about others breaks community. It weaponizes words and makes trust impossible. And in a world where truth is contested and language is weaponized, the ninth word becomes a revolutionary commitment: I will not use my voice to destroy you. I will tell the truth, even when truth is costly.

"You shall not covet..." (Exod. 20:17).

Coveting may seem the most private of sins, but it's perhaps the most dangerous. It poisons the heart with entitlement. It's not merely wanting—it's wanting what belongs to another in a way that erodes peace and gratitude. It turns us inward and away from joy. The final commandment is a window into the interior—the imagination disordered, the heart enslaved to endless wanting. And it shows us that transformation must go all the way down. External compliance is not enough. The heart itself must be renewed.

The Shape of Inhumanity

Each commandment, when kept, affirms something essential about what it means to live as God's image-bearers in the world. And each one, when broken, reveals not just a rule violated but a reflection shattered. Together, they form a kind of anthropology— rooted in worship, lived in community, and sustained by truth.

The commandments do not cage us. They hold open the shape of our freedom. In their light, we do not merely see what to avoid. We see what we are meant to become.

But naming the inhumanity is not the last word. It is the penultimate word. The last word belongs to grace—to the covenant God who did not abandon his broken image-bearers, but came among them, took on their flesh, kept their commandments in their place, and opened the way back to the life for which they were made.

We are not well. But we are not without hope. The signs are broken, but the Sign-maker has come to restore them.

The Semiotic Map Forward

The semiotic mapping in this chapter points in two directions. Backward: toward the world as it has been, toward the accumulated fractures of individual and collective sin. The fractures are real. The pain is real. The work of naming them honestly is not optional if we are to heal.

But the map also points forward: toward the world as it was intended to be, and toward the world as it will one day be again. In the next chapters, we will explore what it looks like to live by the signs when they are honored—the way of life, the holy imagination, the resistance to inhuman systems. And we will arrive, finally, at the One who is himself the fulfillment of every sign: Jesus Christ, in whom every commandment finds its living embodiment, its truest interpretation, its ultimate hope.

For now: the naming is complete. The diagnosis is made. And the door to healing stands open. We have seen ourselves in the X-rays. We have recognized the fractures. We have heard, once again, the ancient voice asking: "What kind of humans will you be?"

The answer is beginning to take shape.

Notes

1. Thomas F. Torrance, *The Mediation of Christ*, rev. ed. (Edinburgh: T&T Clark, 1992), 39. Torrance's framing of sin as broken communion rather than merely broken law is central to his mediatorial Christology.

2. Ellen F. Davis, *Getting Involved with God: Rediscovering the Old Testament* (Cowley Publications, 2001), 24. Davis's insight about idolatry as the worship of false selves resonates with the psychological and theological dimensions of the commandment.

3. Abraham Heschel, *The Sabbath: Its Meaning for Modern Man* (New York: Farrar, Straus and Giroux, 1951), 8.

Chapter 7

The Ten Words and the Way of Life

"The law of the Lord is perfect, reviving the soul." — Psalm 19:7

The Practice

A young musician sits at the piano, eyes on the sheet music. She has been learning this sonata for six months now. In the beginning, it was all labor. Count the measures. Watch the fingers. Start and stop, start and stop. The notation seemed tyrannical— each black dot a demand, each line and space a constraint. Her hands rebelled. Her eyes ached from concentration. The music was not music; it was mathematics.

But something has changed. Last night, as she played through the opening movement alone in the quiet of the evening, the shift came. Her hands found the keys without thinking. The rhythm became as natural as breathing. The counting disappeared into the music itself. What had been external law—the implacable demands of the score—had become something else entirely. It had become voice. The notation, rather than constraining her, had trained her. The discipline had become freedom. She was not playing the music; the music was playing her.

This is what the Ten Words are for. Not to make us mechanical rule-followers who perform obedience by counting steps. Not to reduce human life to rote compliance with an external checklist. But to form us, over years and years of practice, into a people who live the way of love so naturally that it becomes our native tongue. The commandments are not the destination—they are the training that gets us there. They are the scales that, once mastered, disappear into the music itself.

When the Scriptures refer to the Ten Commandments, they often call them not "commandments" but "the Ten Words" (Hebrew: עשרת הדברים, *aseret hadevarim*; Exod. 34:28; Deut. 4:13). Words, not merely laws.

In this chapter, we will trace how the "Ten Words" form a path not only of obedience but of wisdom, shaping a community that embodies the life of God in the midst of a fragmented and fearful world. We will explore how they are not merely regulative—constraining bad behavior—but formative, shaping us into a different kind of people.

This is not a call to nostalgia, nor a summons to legalism. It is an invitation to return to the words that first taught us what it means to be truly human.

The Nature of the "Words"—Revelation Before Regulation

The "Ten Words" are first and foremost acts of revelation. They reveal who God is—the God who liberates, who commands, who covenants. They also reveal who we are called to be: a people who worship rightly, rest faithfully, speak truthfully, honor generationally, and live with dignity before God and each other.

This primacy of revelation changes how we approach the Decalogue. It is not a checklist to be mechanically obeyed; it is an unveiling of reality. In the words of Brevard Childs, "The Decalogue functions as a summary of the whole will of God for Israel, not as a set of minimum standards."[1] Each commandment, then, unveils something essential. The prohibition against idolatry reveals God's uniqueness. The command to honor parents reveals the intergenerational weave of community. The Sabbath reveals the God who rests, and who invites his people to rest in him.

So, obedience to the "words" is not mere compliance; it is alignment with reality. It is to live in truth rather than illusion, in freedom rather than slavery, in love rather than fear.

This is why the psalmist can say, "I delight in your commandments because I love them" (Ps. 119:47). The law is not a burden but a light—a way into life.

The Shape of Life Under the Ten Words

To live under the Ten Words is to inhabit a world structured by covenantal fidelity rather than self-interest. It is to move through life not as isolated individuals but as members of a community bound together by shared allegiance to a common Lord and a common way of life.

The first three words orient us toward God: no other gods, no idols, no misuse of the divine name. Life begins with worship. True human flourishing cannot be separated from true devotion. As Miroslav Volf writes, "To love God with all your heart, soul, and mind, and your neighbor as yourself—this is the whole law. Everything else is commentary, and the commentary exists to help you live the law."[2]

The fourth word—Sabbath—is the hinge between our orientation toward God and our orientation toward each other. Sabbath says: stop. Be still. Know that I am God. And in that knowing, learn to treat yourself and your neighbor as those who are held by Someone greater than productivity demands.

The fifth through tenth words orient us toward each other: honoring parents, protecting life, guarding fidelity, respecting ownership, speaking truthfully, ordering desire. These are not merely social contracts; they are covenantal practices. They are the grammar of a community that takes the image of God in each person seriously.

The Ten Words and the Freedom to Love

One of the great misunderstandings about the Ten Words is that they are fundamentally restrictive—as if their primary purpose is to fence human freedom in. But the opposite is true. The Ten Words are fundamentally liberating.

To have no other gods is to be free from the tyranny of lesser loves. To keep Sabbath is to be free from the tyranny of unending work. To honor parents is to be free from the rootlessness of disconnected individualism. Not to murder, steal, or covet is to be free from the chains of violence, greed, and envy.

The commandments, rightly understood, are not walls but wings. They free us to love—to love God fully, to love neighbors genuinely, to love ourselves honestly. The law is, at its core, a love ethic.

This is why Jesus can summarize the entire law in the double commandment of love (Matt. 22:37-40). He is not replacing the Ten Words; he is revealing their inner logic. The Ten Words are ten dimensions of love—love that worships, rests, speaks truly, honors, protects, and desires rightly.

The Ten Words Written on the Heart

The Old Testament already anticipates that external observance is not enough. The prophets knew that the people needed more than a law to follow—they needed a transformation of desire itself. Jeremiah and Ezekiel both point toward a day when God will write his law not on stone but on the human heart.

"This is the covenant that I will make with the house of Israel after those days, declares the LORD: I will put my law within them, and I will write it on their hearts. And I will be their God, and they shall be my people" (Jer. 31:33).

This is the work of the Holy Spirit. In the new covenant, the Ten Words are not something to be done away with but internalized. They are written on the heart, not as external demands but as interior desires. The person who has the Spirit does not merely obey—they long to obey. They begin to want what God wants.

Paul describes this new reality: "the righteous requirement of the law might be fulfilled in us, who walk not according to the flesh but according to the Spirit" (Rom. 8:4). The Spirit does not make the law unnecessary; the Spirit makes the law possible from within.

Living the Words: Pauline Ethics and Union with Christ

Nijay Gupta's work on Pauline ethics illuminates how Paul understands the new covenant life of the commandments. For Paul, obedience to God's moral will is not a matter of self-generated willpower applied to external law. It is a matter of participation—of being united to Christ by the Spirit and living out from within that union.[3]

When Paul says "I have been crucified with Christ. It is no longer I who live, but Christ who lives in me" (Gal. 2:20), he is describing a transformed anthropology, not merely a changed behavior. The "I" that tries to keep the law by willpower has been crucified. The new self, animated by the indwelling Christ, lives the law from a different center.

This has enormous implications for how we approach the Ten Words. We do not keep them by gritting our teeth. We keep them —or rather, Christ keeps them in us—by growing in our union with the One who already perfectly embodied them. The disciplines of prayer, worship, Scripture, community, and the sacraments are the means by which that union deepens, and through which the Ten Words are progressively written on the heart.

Gupta also emphasizes the communal dimension of this Pauline ethic. Paul's vision of Spirit-empowered life is never individualistic. It is ecclesial—lived out in the body of Christ, with the community as the context and safeguard of faithful discipleship. The Ten Words were given to a community, not to isolated individuals. They describe a communal way of life: a people who together worship rightly, rest together, speak truthfully to one another, protect one another's dignity and possessions and reputations.

Citizens of the Kingdom

Patrick Schreiner's work on the kingdom of God provides a further frame for understanding the Ten Words as a way of life. The kingdom is not merely a future hope; it is a present reality that claims allegiance now. To live by the Ten Words is to live as a citizen of this kingdom—to order one's life by its values, its rhythms, its commitments.[4]

Schreiner emphasizes that the kingdom has a visual quality. It is meant to be seen—in the lives of those who belong to it. When the Ten Words are lived, the kingdom becomes visible. When a community worships the living God alone, rests in trust, honors the elderly, protects the vulnerable, tells the truth at cost, and refrains from covetousness—that community is a sign of the kingdom. The world sees, and wonders. In this sense, to keep the Ten Words is to become a signpost pointing to another world, one where God's rule is absolute and unopposed.

The Ten Words as the Grammar of New Creation

The Ten Words are not only for now—they are for the age to come. Or, more precisely, they are the shape of that age breaking into the present.

The new creation, toward which all of history is moving, will not be lawless. It will be a world where the Ten Words are not reluctantly obeyed but joyfully expressed—a world where there are no other gods because the living God fills all in all; no false witnesses because truth reigns; no coveting because every desire is ordered toward delight in God and neighbor.

In practicing the Ten Words today, we are not merely following ancient rules. We are living as citizens of the coming world, in the present world. We are signs—semiotic events—pointing toward a reality that is already real in Christ, and will one day be fully revealed.

The Ten Words are not only law. They are eschatology. They are a foretaste of the feast to come.

Notes

1. Brevard S. Childs, *The Book of Exodus: A Critical, Theological Commentary* (Philadelphia: Westminster Press, 1974), 397.

2. Miroslav Volf, *A Public Faith: How Followers of Christ Should Serve the Common Good* (Grand Rapids: Brazos Press, 2011), 87.

3. Nijay K. Gupta, *Paul and the Language of Faith* (Grand Rapids: Eerdmans, 2020), 120–145. Gupta's study of Paul's faith language situates participation and transformation within a Pauline anthropology of union with Christ.

4. Patrick Schreiner, *The Kingdom of God and the Glory of the Cross* (Wheaton: Crossway, 2018), 109–130.

Chapter 8

Inhuman Systems and the Ten Words in the Modern World

"The powers of this world promise freedom but deliver chains. Only covenant love can truly set us free." — Walter Brueggemann, Truth Speaks to Power

A woman lay awake at 2 AM, her phone glowing in the darkness. The blue light cast shadows across her face. Scroll. Pause. One more post arrives, a notification chimes, and before her mind can fully register the image, her thumb pulls the next one into view. One more. One more. And one more. Her body lies still in bed, but her mind is in twelve cities simultaneously, reading headlines she will forget by morning, watching videos that end but whose algorithm-suggested cousins continue endlessly.

The phone finally goes dark. The ceiling is there. The quiet is almost strange.

Something is wrong. Not catastrophically wrong—just a low, persistent wrongness. The sense of a hunger that is being fed but not satisfied. Of a life lived at speed, but in circles. A feeling that is not quite sadness, not quite happiness, but a kind of restless numbness. An alertness that leads nowhere.

Pharaoh's world did not need chains to keep its people in line. It just needed to keep them busy. And tired. And wanting. The empire of our day is not built of stone and whips. It is built of screens and algorithms and an economy of endless desire. But its effect is the same: it makes us forget who we are. And it keeps us from rest.

We have traced the semiotic logic of the Ten Words—how they are signs pointing to the deep structure of reality as God designed it. We have seen what it looks like when those signs are honored, and when they are broken. Now we must name the systems—the organized, structural, collective forces—that are designed, whether intentionally or not, to break those signs at scale. These are not merely personal temptations. They are cultural architectures. And resisting them requires more than individual willpower. It requires a community that has been formed by a different imagination.

The Ten Words were given to a people emerging from the brutal machinery of empire. But they were not meant only for ancient Israel. They continue to speak, urgently, to a world that often forgets its true foundations, a world where the logic of Pharaoh persists under new names.

We live today amid powerful systems—economic, technological, political—that shape imaginations, desires, and daily life. These systems often promise freedom, abundance, and connection[1]. And yet, beneath the promises, there runs another current: commodification of persons, erosion of truth, endless stimulation of desire. The empire has not died. It has evolved.

Because of this, we need to explore how the Ten Words confront the inhuman systems of our time. We will trace the return of Pharaoh's logic, the commodification of the human, the loss of Sabbath, the crisis of truth, the disordered desires of consumerism—and finally, how covenantal life rooted in Christ holds out an alternative.

The Decalogue is not a nostalgic relic. It is a prophetic protest. It is the shape of a truly human life—then, now, and in the world to come.

The Return of Empire

Pharaoh's Egypt was defined by fear, anxiety, and the relentless pursuit of control. Production, not persons, was paramount. Memory was suppressed. Time was enslaved. And the vulnerable were expendable whenever their presence threatened the system's smooth operation (Exod. 1:8–22).

This ancient logic did not vanish with Egypt's decline. It merely changed costumes. Throughout history, the machinery of empire has continued to reappear—whether in Babylon, Rome, industrial Europe, or the digital landscapes of the modern world.

Today, we are conditioned to accept that constant expansion is inevitable, that efficiency is always virtuous, that human beings are valuable primarily insofar as they contribute to economic or political power. It is the voice of Pharaoh, now mediated through algorithms and economies, still whispering: produce more, consume more, be more.

Theologian Walter Brueggemann has diagnosed this dynamic with prophetic clarity: "The commodity system is an act of imagination, an act of politics, and an act of theology; it is a religion that forms its practitioners into a certain kind of people."[2] In such a system, exhaustion is normal, anxiety is productive, and persons are means to ends.

Under such pressures, it becomes easy to forget the God who liberates. It is easy to believe that our worth is measured by productivity. It's easy to see others as competitors, obstacles, or means to an end.

Empire lives by amnesia. It thrives when we forget who we are—and whose we are. It demands loyalty to abstractions: to markets, to ideologies, to brands. It colonizes our desires and captures our imaginations.

In the face of such forces, the Ten Words still stand as counter-speech. They tell a different story. They name a different allegiance. They insist that we are not commodities. We are covenant partners. We are creatures made for worship, rest, truth, and community.

To recognize Pharaoh's logic today is the first act of resistance. To remember the God who said, "I am the LORD your God, who brought you out of the land of Egypt, out of the house of slavery" (Exod. 20:2) is the first step toward freedom.

The Ten Words remind us that we are not slaves. We are sons and daughters. And in every age, to remember this truth is itself an act of liberation.

Commodification of the Human

When Scripture proclaims that humanity is made "in the image of God" (Gen. 1:27), it establishes a foundation of sacred worth that no empire, no system, no economic theory can erase. To be human is to reflect divine glory—not to be reduced to utility, efficiency, or profitability.

Yet the commodification of the human has become a defining mark of modern life. Persons are marketed, measured, and monetized. Social media turns identity into brand. Labor markets treat workers as interchangeable parts. Even personal data—our preferences, our habits, our fears—becomes a product bought and sold without our full awareness.

In such a world, the image of God is obscured. Worth is no longer intrinsic but transactional. You are valued not for who you are but for what you produce, how you perform, what you consume.

This is not merely an economic issue. It's a theological crisis. As theologian Willie James Jennings warns, "The commodification of people transforms the very way we imagine bodies, relationships, and community."[3] It reshapes imagination at its roots.

The Ten Words stand firmly against this. "You shall not steal" (Exod. 20:15) is not only about property—it is about honoring the integrity of persons. "You shall not bear false witness" (Exod. 20:16) demands that we see and speak truthfully about others, resisting all systems that reduce persons to data points or demographic targets.

The Sabbath commandment, too, speaks directly against commodification. It insists that human beings are not defined by production. It declares that rest is holy and that dignity is not earned but given.

To live by the Ten Words today is to resist the reduction of human life to commodity. It is to insist that every person—whether productive or weak, visible or hidden, successful or struggling—bears the indelible mark of divine image.

To recover this vision is to recover our own humanity. And it is to bear prophetic witness against the systems that would trade it away for profit.

In semiotic terms, commodification is the corruption of signs. The sign *person*—which properly points to *image-bearer of God, creature of irreducible worth*—is replaced by the sign *unit of production* or *consumer profile*. The meaning is swapped. And when meaning is swapped at this level, the consequences are not merely philosophical—they are lived in bodies, relationships, and communities. The Sabbath commandment re-signs the human: you are not a unit of production. You are a creature of the covenant. The sign is being restored.

Sabbath as Resistance

The Sabbath commandment is one of the most radical aspects of the Ten Words. In a world driven by endless work and constant striving, Sabbath declares that human beings are not machines, not commodities, and not units of economic output. We are creatures made for rest, delight, and communion with God and neighbor.

In Egypt, the Hebrews had no rest. Their value was measured in bricks, quotas, and labor output (Exod. 5:7–19). Pharaoh's economy had no space for Sabbath. It demanded unrelenting productivity. The command to keep the Sabbath, therefore, was an act of resistance, a declaration that Israel's identity was not determined by their economic output but by their covenantal relationship with a God who himself rested.

In our modern context, the pressure to produce, achieve, and consume never sleeps. Work follows us home through laptops and smartphones. Productivity is praised as a virtue without limit. Even leisure is monetized, turned into another industry of consumption.

Walter Brueggemann captures the countercultural power of Sabbath: "Sabbath is a practical divestment so that neighborly engagement, rather than production and consumption, defines our lives."4 It interrupts the frantic pace of empire and re-centers us in God's gift of time.

Keeping Sabbath is not mere legalism. It is a profound act of trust. To cease from work one day a week is to confess that the world is not held together by our effort but by God's grace. It is to witness that our value does not come from endless striving but from covenantal belonging.

Sabbath also restores human dignity. It allows space for worship, for feasting, for relationships, for laughter, for lament. It reminds us that to be human is to be more than what we produce.

In practicing Sabbath today—whether through a full day of rest or through Sabbath principles woven into daily rhythms—we bear witness against the empire of exhaustion. We declare that we are creatures of a generous Creator, not slaves of Pharaoh's machine.

Sabbath is not a retreat from life. It is the recovery of life. And it remains one of the most needed prophetic practices in our hurried, harried, commodified world.

Speech, Truth, and the Crisis of Trust

Words build worlds. Repeat it with me: **Words build worlds**. When speech is distorted, trust collapses, relationships fracture, and community disintegrates. In the ancient world, false witness could destroy families, tribes, and entire peoples. It could justify injustice, inflame violence, and tear apart the sacred fabric of community. In our modern world, the scale and speed of distortion have increased enormously.

The Ninth Word, "You shall not bear false witness against your neighbor" (Exod. 20:16), protects not only individual reputations but the entire fabric of communal life. It guards the ecosystem of trust upon which a just society depends.

In our contemporary world, however, truth is often treated as malleable. Media landscapes, saturated with misinformation and spin, shape public consciousness. Political rhetoric prioritizes winning over truth-telling. Social media amplifies rumors, half-truths, and manufactured outrage. We live, in the words of philosopher Harry Frankfurt, in a post-truth world where "bullshit"—speech indifferent to truth—has become normalized.

The consequences are profound. Without shared trust in language, democracy falters. Communities harden into tribes. Fear replaces dialogue. Cynicism corrodes the common good.

The Ten Words call us back to a different vision—where words are not weapons but bridges, not tools of domination but instruments of fidelity. Truth-telling is not optional. Truth-telling is covenantal.

As theologian Ellen Davis writes, "Truthful speech is a sacrament of community; it enacts and sustains covenant life."[5] To speak falsely is to desecrate that sacrament. To speak truthfully, even at personal cost, is to bear witness to the God who is truth.

In a time of crisis, the Church is called to be a community of honest speech. This does not mean brutalism or cruelty disguised as "truth-telling." It means careful, courageous, compassionate fidelity to reality—about ourselves, about our neighbors, about the world.

To practice truthful speech is to resist the empire of lies. It is to remember that words shape worlds—and to choose to build a world of trust, not suspicion. It is to live as a people who, in every conversation and every confession, remember that we were made by the Word—and that our words must reflect His life.

Desire Disordered

Desire is not, in itself, evil. God made human beings with longing —for communion, for beauty, for meaning. But in a broken world, desire is easily distorted. It twists inward, away from gratitude and generosity, toward envy, competition, and endless craving.

The Tenth Word, "You shall not covet" (Exod. 20:17), addresses this inner reality. Unlike the other commandments, which focus primarily on external acts, the final word shines a light on the secret movements of the heart. It exposes not only what we do but what we want.

In our modern era, the machinery of consumer capitalism depends precisely on disordered desire. Advertising is designed to cultivate dissatisfaction. Algorithms track and intensify our cravings. Products promise not only utility but identity. We are trained to believe that happiness lies just beyond the next purchase, the next achievement, the next experience.

This restless covetousness fuels environmental degradation, economic injustice, and personal despair. It teaches us to view our neighbors not as gifts but as rivals, possessors of what we lack.

The Decalogue's command against coveting is thus a profound act of liberation. It invites us out of the endless churn of acquisition and into the spaciousness of contentment. It reorients us from envy to celebration, from grasping to gratitude.

The apostle Paul understood this deeply. "I have learned in whatever situation I am to be content," he writes (Phil. 4:11). Such contentment is not passive resignation. It is active freedom— freedom from the tyranny of never-enough.

Theologian William Cavanaugh describes consumer society as "a restless pursuit of novelty, a continuous dissatisfaction with what one has."[6] Against this restlessness, the Tenth Word teaches the radical sufficiency of God's provision.

Practicing this commandment means cultivating gratitude as a daily discipline. It means rejoicing in the good of others rather than resenting it. It means choosing generosity over scarcity, simplicity over accumulation.

In a culture that monetizes longing, to be content is to be revolutionary. It is to live as a sign of the kingdom where "they shall hunger no more, neither thirst anymore" (Rev. 7:16). It is to trust that in God's economy, there is enough—enough grace, enough love, enough life—for all.

Hope Amid Ruins

To speak honestly about the inhuman systems of our time is to risk despair. The forces arrayed against covenantal life are massive, sophisticated, and deeply embedded. Consumerism, nationalism, technologism—each promises life but often delivers bondage. Each whispers the old imperial lies: you are what you produce, what you own, what you achieve.

And yet the Ten Words endure. They are not relics gathering dust. They are seeds buried in the soil of a broken world, still bearing fruit.

Living the Ten Words today is an act of stubborn hope. It is choosing to trust that God's covenant faithfulness is deeper than human rebellion, stronger than imperial machinery, and more enduring than the ruins we see around us.

Hope does not deny the brokenness. It names it clearly and then refuses to grant it the final word.

Each time we worship the living God instead of bowing to idols of wealth or nation, we bear witness. Each time we honor the dignity of the neighbor rather than treating them as a rival or resource, we plant a seed. Each Sabbath kept, each truth spoken, each life cherished, each desire disciplined—these are acts of resistance and acts of hope.

We will stumble. We will sometimes forget. The systems around us are designed to make covenant life seem impractical, even impossible.

But the Spirit of the risen Christ breathes new life into tired lungs. He writes the Ten Words deeper into hearts, not as burdens but as songs.

We live between the ruins of the old world and the rising dawn of the new. Our calling is not to triumph in our strength, but to be faithful witnesses—a covenant people whose lives, however imperfect, still echo the music of Mount Sinai and the empty tomb.

"Hope is not a feeling," theologian Fleming Rutledge reminds us[7]. "Hope is a discipline." It is a daily choice to live as if the promises of God are true. It is a daily refusal to let cynicism have the last word.

Notes

1. Walter Brueggemann, *Truth Speaks to Power: The Countercultural Nature of Scripture* (Louisville: Westminster John Knox, 2013), 1.

2. Walter Brueggemann, *The Prophetic Imagination*, 2nd ed. (Minneapolis: Fortress Press, 2001), 4.

3. Willie James Jennings, *The Christian Imagination: Theology and the Origins of Race* (New Haven: Yale University Press, 2010), 58.

4. Walter Brueggemann, *Sabbath as Resistance: Saying No to the Culture of Now* (Louisville: Westminster John Knox, 2014), 45.

5. Ellen F. Davis, *Getting Involved with God: Rediscovering the Old Testament* (Cowley Publications, 2001), 24.

6. William T. Cavanaugh, *Being Consumed: Economics and Christian Desire* (Grand Rapids: Eerdmans, 2008), 34.

7. Fleming Rutledge, *The Crucifixion: Understanding the Death of Jesus Christ* (Grand Rapids: Eerdmans, 2015), 449.

Chapter 9

The Ten Words and the Formation of a Holy Imagination.

"We become what we behold." — G. K. Beale, We Become What We Worship[1]

The Story Before the Rules

It is nine o'clock on a Wednesday evening, and a child is tucked beneath quilts worn soft by generations. The house settles around them — the old wood frame creaking its familiar lullaby. A parent sits on the edge of the bed, worn cloth book in hand, the pages so loved they have softened like skin.

"Once upon a time," the parent begins, "there was a good king who had to go away. But before he left, he gathered his people around him and gave them laws — not laws of fear, but laws of love. 'Keep these," the king said, "not because I will punish you if you don't. Keep them because I love you. Keep them because you are my people, and I am coming back. And when I return, I want to find you living as the ones I know you to be — true, kind, generous, faithful. I want to find you ready. I want to find you free.'"

The child's eyes grow heavy. "Is that real?" comes the drowsy question.

The parent pauses. Sets a hand gently on the small forehead. "More real than anything," the parent whispers. "More real than the walls of this house. More real than the ground beneath us. It's the most real story there is."

The child's breathing deepens. Their fingers, still gripping the edge of the blanket, relax. They fall asleep holding the book.

Long before we can articulate a theology, we are being formed by stories and images. Our imaginations are shaped before our intellects can evaluate what they receive. We drink in narratives like water, and they become part of our very cells. We absorb images like the skin absorbs sunlight, and they shape how we see the world.

This is why the battle for the imagination is so urgent. The empire knows this. It has always known this. It invests enormously — obsessively — in the images and narratives that form our desires. Billboards and algorithms, screens and songs, advertisements and architecture all whisper their story: that you are not enough, that you need more, that your worth is measured by what you possess and what others think of you.

The question before the church is not whether we will form imaginations. We always do. The question is whether we will be as intentional as empire is intentional. Whether we will offer counter-narratives and counter-images with the same creativity, the same persistence, the same conviction.

The battle for human hearts is, at its root, a battle for human imagination. Pharaoh knew this. Rome knew this. Every empire, every system that seeks to dominate rather than liberate understands that lasting control requires more than chains — it requires capturing the imagination. If you can shape what people believe is real, natural, and possible, you can shape everything else.

The Ten Words are not merely regulations. They are acts of re-creation. They carve new grooves in the communal mind, shaping a different way of seeing, yearning, and living. They call forth a holy imagination — one that can see beyond empire's lies to the reality of God's generous, covenantal world.

Let's explore how the Ten Words cultivate such an imagination. We will see how they retrain worship, reorder time, rebuild community, and prepare a people for the world to come.

Without holy imagination, obedience becomes drudgery. With holy imagination, obedience becomes joy.

The Battle for the Imagination

Empire does not merely enslave bodies; it captivates imaginations. Pharaoh did not need to chain every Hebrew individually if he could shape their collective fear, if he could convince them that slavery was the only life possible, that the God of Abraham was too distant to help, and that the bricks must always be laid.

Pharaoh's dream is always a closed system: scarcity rules, competition is necessary, and the only gods worth serving are those that reinforce power.

God's vision, by contrast, is radically open: abundance is possible, mercy triumphs, and every person is an image-bearer.

The Ten Words are given not simply to instruct but to imagine differently. They open a window in the prison walls. They invite a people to see beyond the brick quotas and hierarchies, beyond the consuming appetites and endless anxieties, to a world shaped by covenant love.

The Canadian philosopher Charles Taylor speaks of "social imaginaries" — the unspoken assumptions that shape what a society believes is normal or desirable.[2] The Ten Words offer a holy social imaginary: a world where God alone is God, where time is sacred, where truth is spoken, where every person is cherished.

Every act of obedience to the Ten Words is, therefore, an act of imagination. It is choosing to live as if the kingdom of God is more real than the kingdoms of this world.

We cannot sustain faithfulness without such imagination. Without it, the commandments become brittle duties. With it, they become glimpses of joy.

Thus, the first task of covenant life is not merely better behavior. It is *liberated seeing*.

It is to receive the Ten Words not just as laws, but as windows — windows opening onto a world where God reigns and humanity is free.

Seeing the Kingdom

Patrick Schreiner argues that the kingdom of God has a fundamentally visual quality — it is meant to be seen, not merely believed in abstractly. When Jesus says "the kingdom of God is at hand," he is announcing something that people can observe, witness, and encounter in bodily experience. The blind see, the deaf hear, the lame walk — these are not merely metaphors. They are demonstrations. The kingdom is showing itself.[3]

This visual quality of the kingdom extends to those who belong to it. The risen Jesus tells his disciples, "Let your light shine before others, so that they may see your good works and give glory to your Father who is in heaven" (Matt. 5:16). The covenant community is meant to be a visible sign of the kingdom — something the watching world can observe and wonder at. Not a hidden sect. Not a private spirituality. A public performance of the covenant way.

Disciples, Schreiner argues, are called to see the kingdom (John 3:3) before they can enter it. Sight precedes participation. This is why holy imagination matters so urgently — without eyes trained to see the kingdom, we cannot live as kingdom citizens. Without imagination formed by the covenant story, we cannot embody the covenant way.

The Ten Words form such eyes. They train the imagination to see the world through the lens of God's covenant: to see every person as an image-bearer worth protecting, every moment of rest as a sacred gift, every act of truth-telling as an act of kingdom witness.

To keep the Ten Words is, in a sense, to practice seeing. It is to develop the perceptual habits of the kingdom. It is to learn to notice what God notices, to value what God values, to protect what God protects.

The watching world sees such seeing. It cannot help but notice a people who treat rest as sacred, who tell the truth when lying would profit them, who protect the vulnerable, who honor their parents, who seek fidelity, who refuse to covet. These are not the behaviors of empire. They are visible signs. Narraphors. Stories written in human flesh.

Relearning Worship

At the heart of the Ten Words lies a call to relearn worship — to turn from the gods of empire, fear, and ambition, and to return to the living God who liberates and sustains.

The first commandment is not merely a prohibition: "You shall have no other gods before me" (Exod. 20:3). It is an invitation.

It calls Israel, and us, to imagine life under a different sovereignty — a sovereignty marked not by oppression but by liberation; not by fear but by love.

Relearning worship means asking: What am I actually living for? What captures my attention, my energy, my devotion? In what or whom do I trust when things go wrong?

The liturgical traditions of the church — gathered worship, confession, thanksgiving, preaching, the Lord's Supper — are not merely religious routines. They are imaginative exercises. They rehearse a different story. They re-form the imagination around the reality of God's reign.

Worship is not an escape from the world. It is the place where we remember what the world is really for — and who we are within it.

When we worship rightly, the idol-saturated culture loses its grip. We begin to see the gods of achievement, comfort, and consumption for what they are: small, transient, ultimately empty. And we are reoriented toward the One who is inexhaustible, eternal, and for us.

Imagination is formed by what we behold. This is why the commandment against idolatry is so urgent. Idols deform the imagination. They train us to see small. The living God — revealed in Scripture, present in worship, embodied in Christ — expands the imagination. He trains us to see truly.

Story Before Proposition

Leonard Sweet has proposed that truth is most powerfully communicated not through abstract proposition but through what he calls *narraphor* — the combination of narrative and metaphor that carries meaning experientially.[4] Before we can explain what the kingdom is, we need to show it. Before we can define the covenant, we need to embody it.

This is how Jesus taught. He did not open his ministry with a systematic theology of the kingdom. He told stories. A father runs to embrace a returning son. A woman searches her whole house for a lost coin. A shepherd leaves ninety-nine sheep to find one. These narraphors do not merely convey information — they form imagination. They make the kingdom vivid, embodied, sensory. They work on the listener not as ideas but as visions, as things seen, as patterns recognized in the depths.

The Ten Words, rightly practiced and proclaimed, are narraphors of a kind. A community that keeps Sabbath is telling a story with its life: that time belongs to God, not to the market. A community that refuses false witness is telling a story: that truth can survive even in a world of lies. A community that honors parents is telling a story: that we are embedded in relationships and traditions larger than ourselves. Each commandment, lived, is a parable of the kingdom — a narraphor for the watching world.

When a child watches their parents speak truthfully at cost, they learn something no sermon can teach: that integrity matters more than profit. When they see their community gather on the seventh day to rest instead of work, they absorb a truth about God's abundance that will reshape their entire relationship to time and anxiety. When they witness forgiveness, see property shared, observe respect for life and loyalty in covenant — they are not merely receiving information. They are being formed.

Relearning Time

The Sabbath commandment — "Remember the Sabbath day and keep it holy" (Exod. 20:8) — is, at its core, an invitation to reimagine time.

In the empire's vision, time is a resource to be spent. Every hour should be productive. Rest is at best a recovery period, at worst a waste. The imagination colonized by empire cannot conceive of time as a gift. Time is money. Money is power. Therefore, time is never enough, and we are always behind.

Sabbath breaks this colonization. It declares that time belongs to God, not to the economy. That one day in seven, all productivity stops — not because we have finished, but because we trust the One who holds all things. It is an act of faith written into the calendar.

Abraham Heschel wrote beautifully of the Sabbath as a "palace in time" — a dwelling place of peace that we enter not by achievement but by trust. To keep Sabbath is to practice the art of reception: receiving time as gift, receiving rest as grace, receiving God's presence as the true substance of our days.[5]

But Sabbath also reshapes how we see all of time. When one day is marked as holy, all days are affected. We begin to notice the rhythms of grace embedded in ordinary life — the morning's light, the meal shared with friends, the child's laughter, the evening's quiet. All of creation becomes charged with meaning when we have learned to receive one day as entirely a gift.

The Ten Words form a holy imagination of time — one that refuses the empire's clock and sets our days to a different rhythm. A rhythm that says you are more than your productivity. Your worth is not measured by your output. You exist in a web of grace that precedes you, sustains you, and will continue long after you are gone.

Relearning Community

The second table of the Decalogue — honoring parents, protecting life, guarding fidelity, respecting property, speaking truthfully, ordering desire — is a curriculum in neighborliness. It is training in the art of seeing others as image-bearers rather than obstacles, as members of a covenantal community rather than competitors in a market.

To honor parents is to practice receiving — to acknowledge that we came from somewhere, that we are embedded in a story larger than ourselves, and that gratitude is a form of wisdom.

To refuse to murder is to practice reverence — to look at another human face and see, however faintly, the image of God.

To refuse to steal is to practice respect — to recognize that what belongs to another person is sacred, that their labor, their property, and their dignity cannot be violated without consequence.

To speak truthfully is to practice presence — to show up fully in the relationship, to risk honesty rather than hide behind performance.

To refuse coveting is to practice contentment — to find sufficiency in what we have rather than defining our lack by what others possess.

These are not merely rules. They are practices that form a particular kind of person — a person capable of genuine community, of the "neighborliness" that Walter Brueggemann sees as the alternative to empire's competitive individualism.

Every community faces the choice Brueggemann names: Will we relate to one another as neighbors in covenant, or as competitors in a market? The market says: take what you can, hide what you have, trust no one, protect what's yours. Covenant says something radically different: what belongs to me is held in trust, your need is my call, your dignity is sacred, our survival is mutual.

The Ten Words carve the covenantal imagination into the structures of community life. They are not optional additions to a healthy society. They are the grammar of human flourishing. Without them, we revert to the patterns of domination that empires have always relied upon.

The Church as a Community of Holy Imagination

The church is called to be the community where this holy imagination is cultivated and sustained. It is not merely a religious institution; it is a school of seeing.

In gathered worship, in the reading and preaching of Scripture, in the sacraments, in the practices of prayer and confession and service, the church forms people in the holy imagination of the Ten Words. It rehearses the covenant story. It practices covenant rhythms. It bears covenant witness.

This is not easy. The church exists in the same world as everyone else — subject to the same imperial pressures, the same disordered desires, the same temptations to amnesia. The church fails. It forgets. It sometimes mirrors the empire rather than offering an alternative.

But the Spirit of God is patient. He keeps calling his people back to the covenant vision. He keeps forming, reforming, and restoring holy imagination in communities that are willing to listen, to confess, and to begin again.

This is the deep work of the church. Not merely to help people behave better. But to help people see differently. To recover the capacity to imagine the world as God imagines it. To dream the dreams of the kingdom. To learn to notice grace. To practice receiving. To build lives and communities that bear witness to a different kind of power — the power of love, sacrifice, truth, and covenant fidelity.

Toward the World to Come

Holy imagination is ultimately eschatological. It is the capacity to see not only what is but what will be — to live in the present as if the future of God is already shaping us.

The Ten Words are a foretaste of the age to come — a world where every person freely worships the living God, where time is entirely a gift, where community is wholly covenant, where truth is spoken without fear, where desire is entirely ordered toward joy in God and delight in the neighbor.

In practicing the Ten Words today, we are not merely following ancient rules. We are participating in the inaugurated new creation. We are allowing the future to shape the present. We are being formed by hope.

And hope, formed by holy imagination, does not disappoint.

Even creation is waiting. Waiting for the full restoration of the image-bearers who will tend it with covenantal love. Waiting for the day when the holy imagination becomes the only imagination. When the way of covenant is not a prophetic alternative but the lived reality of all things.

We are not there yet. But we are on the way. And the Ten Words — as signs of the world that is coming — light the path.

Notes

1. G.K. Beale, *We Become What We Worship: A Biblical Theology of Idolatry* (Downers Grove: IVP Academic, 2008), 16–22. Beale's central thesis is that humans are transformed into the likeness of whatever they worship — a principle derived from Old Testament texts on idolatry and their New Testament application.

2. Charles Taylor, *A Secular Age* (Cambridge: Harvard University Press, 2007), 171–172. Taylor defines social imaginaries as "the ways in which people imagine their social existence, how they fit together with others, how things go on between them and their fellows, the expectations that are normally met."

3. Patrick Schreiner, *The Kingdom of God and the Glory of the Cross* (Wheaton: Crossway, 2018), 19–45.

4. Leonard Sweet, *Giving Blood: A Fresh Paradigm for Preaching* (Grand Rapids: Zondervan, 2014), 31–55. Sweet's concept of "narraphor" draws on both narrative theory and conceptual metaphor theory to argue that preaching should be primarily experiential and imagistic before being propositional.

5. Abraham Heschel, *The Sabbath: Its Meaning for Modern Man* (New York: Farrar, Straus and Giroux, 1951), 21.

Chapter 10

Christ the Fulfillment of the Ten Words

"The Law was given through Moses; grace and truth came through Jesus Christ."

— John 1:17

Dawn breaks over the Sea of Galilee. The light comes slow, reluctant, as if the world itself is uncertain whether it should wake. A fisherman stands in the shallow water, his net gathered in his calloused hands. The same net he has cast for thirty years. The same water, the same boat, the same rhythm of work that his father taught him and his father's father before that.

But something happened three years ago that he cannot stop thinking about. A man walked up to the boat one morning — not different from any other morning, except that everything about it was different. The man said two words: Follow me. And the fisherman dropped his net and followed. And everything changed.

Now the man is dead. Crucified. Three days in the tomb. The authorities made sure of it.

The fisherman is watching the dawn again. The water is still. The sky is the color of ash. He doesn't know what to do with his hands. His fingers remember the weight of the net, the pattern of the cast. But there is no net in his hands now. There is nothing.

Then someone on the shore calls out. A voice he knows but does not recognize. Someone calling his name. Calling him to breakfast. Calling him home.

The fisherman turns toward the voice. And what he sees will change everything again.

The resurrection changes the question. Not "what should I do now?" but "who is alive, and what does his life mean for mine?" In Christ, the Ten Words are not finally about obligation. They are about participation — in the life of the One who kept them perfectly, rose from the dead, and now lives in those who belong to him.

The Ten Words find their ultimate meaning not simply in Sinai, but in a hill outside Jerusalem. The voice that thundered from the mountain is the same voice that cried out, "It is finished" (John 19:30). The God who wrote commandments on stone has written himself into flesh and bone.

And now, we will trace how Jesus Christ is the living fulfillment of the Ten Words. We will trace how he embodies, completes, and transfigures them. We will see that the Decalogue is not an ancient contract, now obsolete and discarded. It is a living covenant, now fulfilled and transformed.

The Ten Words, rightly understood, lead not to legalism, nor to despair, but to Christ. They are not burdens to carry alone. They are signposts pointing to the One who carries us.

The Word Made Flesh — From Sinai to Calvary

"And the Word became flesh and dwelt among us, and we have seen his glory, glory as of the only Son from the Father, full of grace and truth" (John 1:14).

The Ten Words, spoken in fire and cloud, find their living echo in the person of Jesus Christ. He is not merely a teacher of the law. He is its embodiment, its goal, its fulfillment. As the early church father Irenaeus wrote: Christ "did not destroy but fulfilled the law."

At Sinai, God spoke his will into the world through commandments etched in stone. In Bethlehem, God spoke his will into the world through a newborn's cry. Both acts are covenantal. Both reveal a God who will not leave his people without direction, without presence, without love.

Jesus does not abolish the law. "Do not think that I have come to abolish the Law or the Prophets," he says. "I have not come to abolish them but to fulfill them" (Matt. 5:17). In his life, the rhythms of the Decalogue find their living expression: he worships the Father alone, he keeps Sabbath in its truest spirit, he honors his earthly parents, he speaks only truth, he never takes what is not his, he loves without covetousness.

And yet he does more. He presses the law deeper into the heart. In the Sermon on the Mount, he teaches that anger is the seed of murder, that lust is the seed of adultery (Matt. 5:21–28). He reveals that the commandments were never about mere behavior modification. They were always about the transformation of the whole person — the mind, the will, the imagination, the heart.

In this way, Christ both fulfills and deepens the Ten Words. He shows that the commandments were never about legalism. They were always about love: love for God, love for neighbor, love that flows from a transformed heart rather than a clenched will.

The journey from Sinai to Calvary is the journey from stone to Spirit, from fear to freedom. As Paul writes, "Now if the ministry of death, carved in letters on stone, came with such glory... will not the ministry of the Spirit have even more glory?" (2 Cor. 3:7–8).

Christ is the living Sinai, the Word in human form, the covenant faithfulness of God walking among us. And in his death, he does not discard the law. He vindicates it by bearing in his body the curse of every commandment broken, the weight of every "you shall not" violated.

At Calvary, the Word made flesh becomes the Lamb slain. Justice and mercy meet. The demands of the Ten Words are not erased —

they are fulfilled in the love that bears all things, believes all things, hopes all things, endures all things.

Sinai and Calvary are not two stories. They are one great covenant, stretching from the thundercloud to the empty tomb, from the stone tablets to the heart of flesh.

In Christ, the Ten Words live.

In Christ, the Ten Words love.

In Christ, the Ten Words save.

Christ's Life as the Perfect Fulfillment of the Ten Words

Consider how each of the Ten Words finds its perfect expression in the life of Christ:

"You shall have no other gods before me." Jesus's whole life was an act of undivided devotion: "My food is to do the will of him who sent me" (John 4:34). He worshipped the Father alone, resisting every temptation to deflect that worship toward lesser things — including his own comfort and survival (Matt. 4:1-11).

"You shall not make for yourself an idol." Christ himself is the "image of the invisible God" (Col. 1:15) — the true and living Image who renders all idols obsolete. In him, the gap between the divine and the human is bridged, not by our construction, but by God's self-giving.

"You shall not take the name of the Lord your God in vain." Jesus speaks truth always, and only truth. "Let what you say be simply 'Yes' or 'No'" (Matt. 5:37). He never weaponizes the divine name for personal advantage or political leverage.

"Remember the Sabbath day and keep it holy." Jesus is Lord of the Sabbath (Mark 2:28). He keeps its spirit perfectly — not in rigid rule-observance but in restoring the rest and wholeness it was always meant to bring (Luke 13:10-17).

__"Honor your father and your mother."__ Jesus honors his earthly parents (Luke 2:51) and cares for his mother even from the cross (John 19:26-27).

__"You shall not murder."__ Jesus, who could have called twelve legions of angels to his defense (Matt. 26:53), lays down his life instead. He is the anti-murderer — the one who absorbs violence rather than perpetuating it.

__"You shall not commit adultery."__ Jesus is the faithful Bridegroom, whose love for his church is unconditional, unending, and self-sacrificial (Eph. 5:25-27).

__"You shall not steal."__ Jesus takes nothing from anyone. Even his burial shroud is borrowed (John 19:41). He gives everything — his body, his blood, his very self.

__"You shall not bear false witness."__ "I am the way, the truth, and the life" (John 14:6). He is Truth incarnate. Every word he speaks is reality disclosed.

__"You shall not covet."__ Jesus, "though he was in the form of God, did not count equality with God a thing to be grasped" (Phil. 2:6). He is the anti-coveter — the one who, possessing all things, empties himself for the sake of others.

The Cross and the Ten Words — Mercy for the Lawbreakers

At Calvary, Christ does not merely model the Ten Words. He bears the consequence of their violation.

Every broken commandment has a cost. When creation is disordered by idolatry, by violence, by falsehood, by theft, by covetousness — that disorder does not simply dissolve. It accumulates. It becomes a weight that crushes. Paul names this weight the "curse of the law" (Gal. 3:13) — the consequence of the gap between what we were made for and what we have done.

Christ on the cross is God's answer to that accumulated weight. "Christ redeemed us from the curse of the law by becoming a curse for us" (Gal. 3:13). Every commandment broken in human history finds its answer there — not in punishment meted out to the guilty, but in the willing substitution of the Innocent for the guilty.

This is grace. Not cheap grace — not grace that ignores the seriousness of sin and inhumanity. But the grace that names the full weight of the problem and enters it. Grace that costs everything.

The Cross as the Fulfillment of Every Commandment

Michael Gorman's concept of cruciformity — the idea that the cross reveals and embodies the very character of God — provides a profound lens for understanding Christ's fulfillment of the Ten Words. For Gorman, the cross is not merely a transaction (punishment transferred) or a demonstration (love shown). It is the self-disclosure of God — the revelation of what God has always been like, now made visible in the most extreme possible form.

In the cross, every commandment is fulfilled simultaneously and completely. Christ worships the Father alone, even when divine silence is all he receives ("My God, my God, why have you forsaken me?" — Matt. 27:46). He speaks only truth, even when the truth condemns him. He refuses to murder, even when violence would have been justified. He does not covet — "Father, into your hands I commit my spirit" (Luke 23:46) — releasing everything. He honors the covenant even unto death — "It is finished" (John 19:30).

The cross, for Gorman, is also the pattern of Christian life — cruciformity is the shape of authentic discipleship, the living out of the Ten Words in the key of self-giving love. Christians do not merely admire the cross; they are conformed to it. "Anyone who wants to be my disciple must deny himself, take up his cross, and follow me" (Mark 8:34).[1]

This cruciform reading of the commandments transforms how we understand obedience. Keeping the Ten Words is not a matter of

performance or compliance; it is a matter of dying and rising with
Christ — dying to the self-centered distortions that break the
commandments, and rising to the other-centered love that fulfills
them.

Gorman also develops the concept of *theosis* — participation in
the divine nature (2 Pet. 1:4) — as the eschatological goal of the
Christian life. Not absorption into the divine, but transformation
into the image of the God who is cruciform love. This is the end
toward which the Ten Words have always been pointed: a people
who bear the image of God so fully that they reflect the cruciform
love of Christ in every dimension of their lives.[2]

Resurrection and the New Covenant Community

The resurrection changes everything. Christ rises not merely as
proof that he survived death, but as the firstfruits of the new
creation (1 Cor. 15:20) — the beginning of the world made new,
the world in which the Ten Words are no longer the grammar of
an aspirational community but the living, joyful expression of
transformed persons.[3]

The risen Christ breathes the Holy Spirit into his disciples (John
20:22) — a new Pentecost, a new Sinai. Where God once wrote the
commandments on stone tablets, he now writes them, by his
Spirit, on the tablets of human hearts (2 Cor. 3:3). The new
covenant community, empowered by the Spirit, is called to
embody the Ten Words not as a legal obligation but as a living
witness to the resurrection's power.

The Day the Revolution Began

N.T. Wright argues that the resurrection is not the escape of Jesus
from the world, but the beginning of the world's renewal. "On
Easter morning," Wright writes, "something happened in and to
the physical world" — the first particle of new creation came into
being. The risen Christ is not a ghost who has left the old world
behind; he is the embodiment of the new world breaking into the
old.[4]

This has profound implications for understanding the Ten Words. If the resurrection marks the beginning of new creation, then the commandments are not merely the rules of the old covenant order. They are the constitution of the new creation — the description of what fully renewed human life will look like, expressed now in incomplete but genuine form by those who have been united to the risen Christ.

To keep Sabbath in the resurrection age is not to replicate an ancient Jewish practice. It is to embody the rest of the new creation — the rest that the risen Christ has inaugurated. To refuse false witness is not merely to follow an ethical rule; it is to participate in the truthfulness of the resurrection world, where death's last lie ("this is the end") has been exposed.

The revolution that began on Easter morning is still in progress. And the Ten Words are among its primary instruments — the practical, daily, embodied ways in which the new creation is proclaimed and practiced in the midst of the old.

Union with Christ — Living the Ten Words from Within

Paul's vision of the Christian life is captured in a single extraordinary sentence: "I have been crucified with Christ. It is no longer I who live, but Christ who lives in me" (Gal. 2:20).

This is not mystical individualism. It is a description of what happens when a person is incorporated into Christ through faith — they receive not only forgiveness but a new identity, a new center, a new animating life. And that life, the life of the One who perfectly kept every commandment, is now the power from which Christian obedience flows.

We do not keep the Ten Words by heroic self-effort. We keep them — or rather, Christ keeps them in us — by growing in our union with the One who lived them perfectly and who now lives within us by the Spirit. The disciplines of prayer, Scripture, worship, and community are the means by which that union deepens, and through which the Ten Words are progressively written on the heart.

Christ as the Goal and Glory of the Ten Words

The Ten Words are not ends in themselves. They are arrows — and they all point to Christ.

They point to him because he is their fulcrum and fulfillment. They point to him because in him, the commandments are not burdens but invitations — to participate in the life of the One who lived them perfectly and who lives in those who trust him.

To obey the Ten Words is not to earn anything — not favor, not standing, not security. It is to participate in the life of Christ. It is to say yes, with our choices and our bodies and our daily rhythms, to the reality that he has already inaugurated.

The Ten Words are not the end of the journey. Christ is. And the Ten Words, rightly understood, are not chains but a road — a road that leads, through him, to the fullness of what we were created to be.

Notes

1. Michael Gorman, *Cruciformity: Paul's Narrative Spirituality of the Cross* (Grand Rapids: Eerdmans, 2001), 4–15. Gorman's concept of 'cruciformity' describes the pattern of Christ's self-giving love as the shape of God's own character, now visible in the cross.

2. Michael Gorman, *Inhabiting the Cruciform God: Kenosis, Justification, and Theosis in Paul's Narrative Soteriology* (Grand Rapids: Eerdmans, 2009), 9–39. Gorman develops the concept of 'theosis' as participation in the cruciform divine nature.

3. N.T. Wright, *The Day the Revolution Began: Reconsidering the Meaning of Jesus's Crucifixion* (New York: HarperOne, 2016), 337–360. Wright argues that the resurrection is not the evacuation of the physical world but the beginning of its renewal.

4. N.T. Wright, *Surprised by Hope: Rethinking Heaven, the Resurrection, and the Mission of the Church* (New York: HarperOne, 2008), 250–270. Wright's treatment of resurrection as 'first-fruits' of the new creation shapes his understanding of Christian ethics and vocation.

Chapter 11

Becoming Human Again

He who began a good work in you will bring it to completion at the day of Jesus Christ. — Philippians 1:6

The Door Stands Open

The journey had been long. Longer than anticipated. Longer, perhaps, than should have been possible. But the figure making its way down the familiar street—slowly, uncertainly, as if each step were a question being asked of the world—knew the way home by the smallest details.

The corner where the old oak had split from lightning stood witness. The gate that hung crooked on its hinges creaked in recognition. And then, unmistakably, the smell: bread. Someone had been baking.

The windows of the house were lit. Not with the harsh light of accident or necessity, but with a warm, expectant glow that seemed to suggest the lights had been waiting. The wanderer's pace quickened, but not from joy—from something more complicated. Fear, perhaps. Or the strange vertigo of homecoming.

The hand reaching for the door trembled. A speech had been prepared. It was a good speech. Humble. Contrite. Carefully constructed to earn back what had been forfeited. It began with "Father, I have sinned." The words were ready. They had been ready for miles.

But the door opened before the knock could land.

And in that open door stood the one who had been waiting. Not standing in judgment. Not arms crossed. Not even standing at all, but already moving. Running, actually. Running down the road. Running as if he had been watching from the moment the child first left, watching the road every day since, waiting for the distant figure to become clear.

The speech never came. It didn't matter. The embrace came first. The robe. The ring. The feast. The father was not receiving a servant back into service. He was receiving a lost child home to joy.

This is the Bible's best picture of what God is doing with humanity.

Not waiting in silence to administer judgment. Not standing in the doorway with a checklist, preparing to conduct a performance review. Not watching to see if we measure up. Running. Always running. Racing down the road, watching for us with the intensity of one who has been keeping watch from the beginning, and embracing us before we have finished our speech.

The Ten Words are not the conditions for this homecoming. They are not the price of admission to the feast. They are the shape of the life we return to. They are what it looks like when we are finally, truly, home. They are the grammar of covenant love, spoken into a world that has forgotten what home even means.

And the door stands open.

The Ten Words were given to call a people, and a world, back to life. They still do.

Not merely rules. Not relics. Not a museum piece of ancient religion. They are the sounds of a covenant God speaking life over a humanity that had forgotten what life even was.

The Ten Words are about remembering—about remembering who we were meant to be. About remembering the God who made us, who rescued us, and who still calls us home.

But memory alone is not enough. We need reformation. We need resurrection. And so the Ten Words point us beyond themselves— to Christ, the true Word, the living image of the humanity we have lost and are being restored to.

Let us walk this journey one more time.

The Long Forgetting

To forget God is to forget ourselves. This has been humanity's long sorrow. It is not a sudden rebellion, but a slow amnesia. We drift. We compromise. We exchange the truth of God for a lie, the freedom of love for the chains of fear, the joy of covenant for the tedium of performance.

Adam and Eve did not simply break a rule—they broke a relationship. And ever since, humanity has wandered east of Eden, building towers, founding empires, forging idols, seeking life and finding only shadows. The long forgetting is not only a theological fact. It is a personal wound. Every human heart knows the ache of alienation and the gnawing sense that something is not right, that we were made for more than this.

The Ten Words are given into this ache. They are spoken not to condemn, but to call. They are a covenantal declaration that there is a way home. It screams to the world that exile is not the end of the story.

And yet even when the Ten Words are given, the forgetting continues. Israel forgets. The Church forgets. We forget.

In the daily pressures of work, in the anxious swirl of politics, in the seductive lull of consumerism, we lose sight of the holy story. We shrink our imaginations to fit the empires of this world.

But the Ten Words endure. They are the memories of a covenant written in the language of life. They are the call of a God who refuses to forget his people, even when they forget him. They are, still today, an invitation to remember.

Christ, the True Human

The answer to the long forgetting is not human willpower, not moral reformation, not a renewed commitment to try harder. The answer is a Person.

Jesus Christ is the True Human—the one in whom the image of God is fully and perfectly expressed. "He is the image of the invisible God, the firstborn of all creation" (Col. 1:15). He is not merely a good example of how to live. He is the living reality of what humanity was always meant to be.

In Christ, we see what the image of God looks like when it is fully expressed. We see a person who worships rightly, loves truly, speaks faithfully, rests in trust, honors the vulnerable, and gives himself away without reservation. Every commandment is, in him, not a constraint but a joy—the natural expression of a life lived in perfect union with the Father.

And in him, we are being made into that same image. "We all, with unveiled face, beholding the glory of the Lord, are being transformed into the same image from one degree of glory to another" (2 Cor. 3:18). The process is not instantaneous. It is the slow, faithful work of a lifetime, sustained by the Spirit and grounded in the community of faith.

Learning to Walk Again

Becoming human again is not a dramatic moment. It is a daily discipline.

It begins in the small things: in choosing truthful speech when a lie would be more convenient, in honoring a parent when respect has grown difficult, in resting when the culture demands one more hour of productivity, in resisting covetousness when envy whispers its familiar names.

These small acts of covenant faithfulness are not trivial. They are not mere moral hygiene. They are the training of the heart—the slow re-formation of desire and imagination toward the life for which we were made.

The Christian tradition has long understood this as the practice of virtue—the habitual inclination toward the good that comes from repeated acts of right living. The Ten Words are the school of virtue. They teach us, over and over, to orient ourselves toward God and toward the neighbor. And gradually—not all at once, but genuinely—we change.

We learn to walk again. We learn to see again. We learn to love again.

A Community of Hope

We do not walk this road alone. Becoming human again is not a private project; it is a communal vocation.

The church is the community of those who are, together, in the slow process of recovery. It is not a community of the fully healed, but of the honestly broken who have found, together, the way toward healing. It is a community of practice—where the habits of the Ten Words are cultivated together, sustained by shared worship, shared Scripture, shared service, and shared hope.

This community is not perfect. It forgets. It fails. It sometimes resembles the very empires it is called to resist. But the Spirit of the risen Christ keeps calling it back. He keeps forming, reforming, and restoring.

And in its best moments, the community of faith is a sign of what is coming—a glimpse of the fully renewed humanity, bearing God's image without distortion, living in covenant without betrayal, loving without reserve.

The Community That Keeps the Signs

Michael Gorman reminds us that the church is called to be a "cruciform community"—a community whose shared life embodies the pattern of Christ's self-giving love.[1] This means that the church's common practices are not merely religious activities; they are political acts. They are saying to the watching world: there is another way to be human.

N.T. Wright goes further: the church is the "pilot project" of new creation.[2] It is not meant to be a refuge from the world but a demonstration project within the world—showing what human community looks like when it is ordered by the covenant love of the risen Christ rather than the competitive logic of empire.

The Ten Words, practiced in community, become visible. They are signs—semiotic events in Leonard Sweet's language—that point beyond themselves to the reality of the kingdom.[3] When a church community practices Sabbath together, it is telling the story of a God who provides and rests. When it practices honest speech in conflict, it is telling the story of a God who is truth. When it cares for the elderly and the widow and the immigrant, it is telling the story of a God who sees the vulnerable.

These are not primarily programs. They are embodied testimony. They are the community keeping the signs.

Toward the Feast

The Ten Words are not the end of the story. They are the road, not the destination.

The destination is a feast.

In the Scripture, the consummation of all things is described as a wedding banquet, a feast of abundance, a table set for all people (Rev. 19:9; Matt. 8:11; Isa. 25:6-8). The Ten Words point toward a world where the table is set and everyone has a place.

In that world, there will be no need for "You shall not steal"—because there will be no poverty, no scarcity, no grasping. No need for "You shall not murder"—because death will be no more. No need for "You shall not bear false witness"—because deception will have perished in the light of the One who is Truth.

The Ten Words are the grammar of a world still being made. They are the shape of the freedom that is coming. And they are the invitation, today, to begin living in that freedom now.

Come and eat. The table is being set.

The journey home is almost over.

And the door stands open.

Living Signs

We began this book with signs. With the observation that creation is readable—that God has written meaning into the fabric of things, and that the Ten Words are among the most important signs he has given.

We end with the observation that we ourselves are meant to become signs.

As we are formed by the Ten Words, as we grow in union with Christ, as we practice the rhythms of covenant life together—we become readable. Our lives begin to point beyond themselves, toward a reality that most of the world cannot yet see. We become signs of the coming kingdom. We become, in Paul's remarkable phrase, "a letter from Christ... written not with ink but with the Spirit of the living God, not on tablets of stone but on tablets of human hearts" (2 Cor. 3:3).

This is the goal. Not perfect commandment-keeping. Not faultless performance. But a life that is, gradually, unmistakably, legibly human—human in the way that Christ was human, human in the way that we were always designed to be.

The long forgetting is being reversed. The broken signs are being restored. The image is being renewed.

Come. Let us be, together, the sign of the One who is coming.

And let it be Jesus. Only Jesus. Always Jesus.

Notes

1. Michael Gorman, *Becoming the Gospel: Paul, Participation, and Mission* (Grand Rapids: Eerdmans, 2015), 44–76. Gorman develops the idea of the church as a 'cruciform community' whose corporate life embodies the pattern of Christ's self-giving love.

2. N.T. Wright, *Surprised by Hope: Rethinking Heaven, the Resurrection, and the Mission of the Church* (New York: HarperOne, 2008), 204–235. Wright's description of the church as a 'pilot project' of new creation captures the inaugurated-eschatological dimension of Christian community.

3. Leonard Sweet, *Nudge: Awakening Each Other to the God Who's Already There* (Colorado Springs: David C Cook, 2010), 19–37. Sweet articulates the church as a 'semiotic community'—a community whose common life becomes readable as a sign pointing toward the kingdom of God.

Appendix

Semiotic Mapping of the Decalogue

This appendix is for readers who want to go deeper into the semiotic framework introduced in Chapter 1 and referenced throughout the book. It is not required reading—the main chapters stand on their own. But for those who want to explore the semiotic dimensions of the Decalogue more fully, what follows may prove illuminating.[1]

Semiotics is the study of signs and meaning—of how marks, words, symbols, and actions point beyond themselves to realities they represent. Charles Sanders Peirce, Ferdinand de Saussure, and Umberto Eco each contributed to its development as a discipline.[2] But the insight that meaning is sign-mediated is as old as the biblical tradition itself. God communicates through signs: the rainbow, the Passover lamb, the burning bush, the empty tomb. The ultimate Sign is Christ himself—"the image of the invisible God" (Col. 1:15), the Sign that interprets all other signs.

The Ten Commandments are a coherent sign-system. Each commandment is a sign with a positive valence (what it affirms about covenantal human life) and a negative valence (what its violation reveals about the collapse of that life). The table below maps both dimensions.

What Are Signs?

A sign, in the semiotic sense, is something that stands for something else. The word "tree" is a sign—it points to the thing itself. A photograph is a sign—it represents a moment in time. A traffic light is a sign—red points to "stop," green to "go." But signs are never transparent. They carry assumptions, histories, and meanings that are culturally embedded.

In the theological tradition, semiotics become even more important. God does not communicate only through propositions. He communicates through creation itself—through what theologians call "natural revelation." The heavens declare the glory of God. A seed speaks of death and resurrection. The family structure speaks of covenant love. These are signs, and they are readable.

The Ten Commandments are part of this semiotic order. They are not arbitrary rules. They are signs that point to the deep structure of covenantal reality—to what human flourishing looks like, and what human collapse looks like. They are never innocent. They stand for something—and what they stand for forms the fabric of our reality.

The Two Arcs of the Decalogue

The Decalogue divides naturally into two movements:

Commandments 1–4 define vertical fidelity—humanity's relation to God. Their violation distorts worship, meaning, and the cosmic grammar of reality itself. When we abandon God, we do not simply lose a belief; we fracture the entire symbolic order by which life makes sense.

Commandments 5–10 define horizontal fidelity—humanity's relation to other humans. Their violation erodes community, justice, and love. When we steal, murder, betray, or lie, we are not simply breaking an isolated rule; we are tearing at the fabric of the communion for which we were made.

Both arcs are essential. Both point to the deepest truths about what it means to be human. And both are being restored in Christ.

The Semiotic Mapping Table

The table below presents each of the Ten Commandments, with two columns: what is affirmed when the sign is honored (the positive dimension) and what is revealed when the sign is broken (the negative dimension, showing the collapse of covenantal humanity).

Commandment	Sign Honored (Positive)	Sign Broken (Negative / Inhumanity)
1. You shall have no other gods	God is sufficient; humans are worshipping creatures	Spiritual alienation, idolatry, the disordered soul
2. You shall not make idols	God is infinite, beyond manipulation	Domesticated theology, false self, manageable religion
3. You shall not take the name of God in vain	Language is sacred; God's name carries reality	Hollow speech, manipulation, erosion of meaning
4. Remember the Sabbath day	Humans are creatures, not machines; time is gift	Exhaustion, loss of creaturely identity, dehumanizing productivity
5. Honor your father and mother	Community has roots; identity is intergenerational	Rootlessness, historical amnesia, severed covenant continuity
6. You shall not murder	Every human bears God's image; life is sacred	Dehumanization, violence, the erasure of the image
7. You shall not commit adultery	Covenant love is faithful; promises can be kept	Broken trust, covenant rupture, relational disintegration
8. You shall not steal	Others' dignity and property are sacred	Exploitation, disregard for human dignity, injustice

| 9. You shall not bear false witness | Truth grounds community; words build worlds | Manipulation, fractured community, weaponized language |
| 10. You shall not covet | God's provision is sufficient; gratitude is possible | Restless dissatisfaction, rivalry, disordered desire |

Interpretive Reflection

When the signs are honored, life flourishes. The commandments create a coherent symbolic world—a world of right worship, truthful speech, sacred rest, honored ancestry, protected life, faithful covenant, respected dignity, reliable witness, and grateful desire. These are not disconnected virtues; they form an interlocking system of meaning that holds the universe together.

When the signs are broken, meaning collapses. The commandment against stealing is not a rule meant to prevent shoplifting. It is a sign that others' property and dignity are sacred. When that sign is broken—when we steal, exploit, or take what is not ours—we are declaring that human dignity is not sacred, that exploitation is permissible, that the world operates by the logic of power rather than the logic of covenant. The brokenness cascades.

This is why Paul Ricoeur eloquently writes: "Evil is not merely the absence of good; it is the distortion of the signs by which life and meaning are mediated."[3] Evil is not simple negligence. It is active, deliberate sign-breaking. It is the distortion and weaponization of the very systems through which God communicates truth.

But there is a third trajectory, made possible in Christ: the world of restored signs.

The Restored Signs

In Christ, the broken signs are being repaired. The idolater becomes a true worshipper. The liar becomes a truth-teller. The covetous heart becomes a grateful one. The murderous impulse gives way to sacrificial love. The adulterer is restored to covenant fidelity. These restorations are imperfect in this age—but they are real.

The Spirit of Christ is at work, repairing the sign-system from within. Where the signs were broken, they are being made readable again. Where language was weaponized, it is being restored to truth. Where covenants were shattered, they are being healed. Where life was diminished, it is being honored.

The church, at its best, is a community of restored signs—a place where the Decalogue is lived not as law but as life, not as burden but as joy, not as external constraint but as the natural expression of hearts being renewed in the image of Christ.

This is the hope of the book. Not that we will achieve perfection. Not that the signs will ever be perfectly honored in this age. But that the signs, in Christ, are being renewed—and that the world they point toward is more real, more true, and more worth living for than the broken world we inhabit.

Notes

1. Leonard Sweet, Giving Blood: A Fresh Paradigm for Preaching (Grand Rapids: Zondervan, 2014), 40–55. Sweet's application of semiotics to theological communication.

2. Umberto Eco, A Theory of Semiotics (Bloomington: Indiana University Press, 1976), 7.

3. Paul Ricoeur, The Symbolism of Evil (New York: Harper & Row, 1967), 156.

Acknowledgements

There are people without whom this book simply would not exist, and I want to take a moment to name them.

My parents, Buster and Margaret Phillips.

They were extraordinarily supportive of everything I pursued in life. They gave me the foundation I needed as a child and continued to cheer me on long into adulthood. They are in Heaven now, and I wish with all my heart they could hold this book in their hands.

My wife, Claire.

She read the first draft and encouraged me deeply. She has walked with me through adoption, through loss, through new ventures — never wavering. She is a remarkable wife and mother, and I am more grateful for her than words on a page can adequately express.

My doctoral mentor, Leonard Sweet.

He taught me to see my faith differently — to understand that everything is caught up in Jesus, and to read the signs embedded in Scripture. This book bears his fingerprints. I hope it makes him proud.

My longtime friend, Todd Littleton.

He read an early draft and offered wise counsel on how to proceed. His probing questions made this a better book than it would have been without him.

My sixth-grade teacher, Linda Green.

It is rare to remain in contact with a teacher from that season of life, but she has always held a special place for me. She read this draft, offered generous encouragement, and I cannot imagine having moved forward without it.

Thanks to you all!

About the Author

Dr. David Phillips holds a Bachelor of Science in Computer Information Systems, a Master of Divinity, and a Doctor of Ministry, completing his doctoral studies under the mentorship of Dr. Leonard Sweet.

His ministry has taken him across the American South and Mid-Atlantic. He has replanted and revitalized churches in Louisiana and Delaware, and also served as pastor in Georgia, where he currently resides.

Dr. Phillips has also served in higher education, teaching at the bachelor's, master's, and doctoral levels at multiple colleges and seminaries.

Alongside his life in ministry, Dr. Phillips has spent more than two decades at the intersection of technology and leadership. Since 1997, he has worked as a full-stack developer, project manager, and technical product manager, and has founded and operated a technology consulting company. This dual vocation — theologian and technologist — has given him a distinctive vantage point from which to observe the systems that shape modern human life, and to ask what it might mean to recover something more fully human within them.

He is also the author of *Kept, Holy Rewired*, and *Jesus Was a Baptist*.

9 798234 020550